POCKET
DICTIONARY

FOR THE STUDY OF
NEW TESTAMENT GREEK

MATTHEW S.
DeMOSS

InterVarsity Press
Downers Grove, Illinois

InterVarsity Press
P.O. Box 1400, Downers Grove, IL 60515-1426
World Wide Web: www.ivpress.com
E-mail: mail@ivpress.com

InterVarsity Press® is the book-publishing division of InterVarsity Christian Fellowship/ USA®, a student movement active on campus at hundreds of universities, colleges and schools of nursing in the United States of America, and a member movement of the International Fellowship of Evangelical Students. For information about local and regional activities, write Public Relations Dept., InterVarsity Christian Fellowship/USA, 6400 Schroeder Rd., P.O. Box 7895, Madison, WI 53707-7895, or visit the IVCF website at <www.ivcf.org>.

Cover illustration: Daryl Benson/Masterfile

ISBN 0-8308-1464-7

Printed in the United States of America ∞

Library of Congress Cataloging-in-Publication Data

DeMoss, Matthew S., 1969-
    Pocket dictionary for the study of New Testament Greek/Matthew S. DeMoss.
      p. cm.
    ISBN 0-8308-1464-7 (alk. paper)
    1. Greek language, Biblical—Dictionaries—English.   2. Bible. N.T.—Language, style—Dictionaries.   I. Title.

PA881 .D46 2001
487'.4—dc21

                                           2001024839

16	15	14	13	12	11	10	9	8	7	6	5	4
13	12	11	10	09	08	07	06	05				

To my parents,
Tom and Gail DeMoss,
with gratitude and affection

CONTENTS

Preface

Those who undertake to study the New Testament in its original language, and engage others who are likewise involved in the interpretive task, enter a labyrinth of methods, concepts and terminology. This book is about the terminology. It is primarily for students—a companion volume to help them use the standard tools, understand the jargon and survive academic life.

The majority of the entries pertain to language study: some are terms from traditional grammar and literary analysis; others are peculiar to learning Koine; still others are derived from modern linguistic studies. This book also contains a corpus of terms pertaining to textual criticism.

Not only are these two areas—learning the language (as well as the metalanguage) and establishing the text—foundational for biblical study, they are fertile ground for troublesome words. Originally the draft for this book contained only these two entry-types; however, in the writing process I realized the advantage for the student of including terms from other subfields, such as Gospel studies, which are also difficult and forbidding to newcomers.

Exegesis of the Greek New Testament is part of a larger constellation of disciplines. I readily acknowledge there is an enormous body of terminology, vital to trafficking in the literature and studying the New Testament, which for one reason or another exceeds the scope of this book. This includes biographical and geographical terms, often the mainstay of handbooks and Bible dictionaries. Likewise words related to all aspects of background (social, cultural, historical, religious, political and so on), including extracanonical writings, are not attended to. These words and the complex themes associated with them deserve, and indeed have been given (repeatedly), their own treatment elsewhere. Furthermore, there is little in this book from theology and biblical studies generally, although there is a handful of words pertaining to hermeneutics. A number of specialized tools already in print deal particularly with these subjects.

Moreover, I have chosen not to include bibliographic data. Not only would the work have increased in size considerably, I would have had to choose between, on the one hand, steering the reader to a small strand of the literature, or on the other hand, providing a kind of rambling historical overview. For some terminology (e.g., form-critical categories) it would be natural to trace chronologically how authors have used certain words; but in terms of pedagogy, I question the value of such a "definition" for the new student. No doubt if I had chosen such a presentation, I would be more likely to concur with Renaissance scholar J. J. Scaliger, who said that "the worst criminals should be neither executed nor sentenced to forced labor, but should be condemned to compile dictionaries, because all the tortures are included in the work."[1] In order to provide succinct, readable definitions, such as you would find in a standard desk dictionary, I have avoided historical/bibliographical entries.

This raises the issue of competing definitions. It may come as a surprise to the new student that in grammatical and exegetical tools, writers adopt certain nomenclature and discard other terms. Neologisms are widespread too. The fact that terms have been, and continue to be, used differently makes composing definitions rather challenging. It is not simply that writers use different terms for the same phenomenon (though they do this) or the same term for different language features (though they do this too); rather there is often overlapping usage or a slightly different signification given to a term. Also, as is frequently the case in discussions of grammatical features, certain writers subsume one or more categories under a single heading. What I have tried to do in such cases is compose definitions that encapsulate the essence of a term so that the student can construe the basic idea. For terms whose meanings were too disparate to accommodate this approach, I have provided the definitions one after the other.

For entries that can be identified by more than one term, I have

---

[1]Cited in Jonathon Green, *Chasing the Sun: Dictionary Makers and the Dictionaries They Made* (New York: Henry Holt & Co., 1996), pp. 9-10.

included the definition just once in order to conserve space; the other "entries" merely serve as pointers to the main listing. The main headwords were chosen based on widespread usage and only rarely because of personal preference.

I chose to make the entries definitional rather than descriptive, although in some cases this is easier said than done (e.g., defining *feminine* or *masculine* when Hellenistic Greek employed grammatical gender). I have done this not only because of lexicographical precedent but also because it seems the best approach from a pedagogical standpoint.

This book would not have been possible without the assistance of a number of kind people. I would like to express gratitude to Darrell Bock, Buist Fanning, Paul Felix, Robert Gundry, Grant Osborne, Daryl Schmidt, Tom Schreiner, Moisés Silva, Jay Smith, Dan Wallace and Roy Zuck, all of whom believed in this project when it was still in embryonic form. Any shortcomings of this present work belong entirely to me. Thanks are also due to Frances Gannon, Terra Lewis, Kristy Kegerreis, and Helen Beidel (the "Latin ladies") for their assistance with the abbreviations list. I am also grateful to InterVarsity for taking this project, especially Dan Reid and his expert editorial eye. I am also indebted to Susan Carlson Wood for her excellent work of red-flagging and fine-tuning the definitions, and Charles Powell for looking over the penultimate manuscript. Lastly, I am very appreciative of my girls, Lori and Heather, who allowed me the time needed to research and write.

Cross-References

This pocket dictionary is cross-referenced using the following system:

An asterisk before a term or phrase indicates that it appears elsewhere in the book as a separate entry. Within an entry, only the first occurrence of a term or phrase is cross-referenced. When two related terms occur within the same phrase, the more specific term or phrase is cross-referenced.

See also references within or at the end of a definition are followed by the name of another entry that provides additional information.

An alphabetized entry title with no definition is followed by *see* and the name of the entry under which the definition will be found.

A

a fortiori. Lat. "from a stronger [reason or argument]." The term is similar to the expression "all the more" and refers to a conclusion that can be drawn with greater logical necessity than a previous one. *See also qal wahomer.*

ablative. *adj.* Denoting separation or the idea of movement away from something. —*n.* An ablative word; or one of the *cases in the *eight-case system (Lat. *ablativus,* "pertaining to removal from").

ablaut. *n.* Alteration of the vowels of words indicating a change of *case, *tense, etc., as in *swim, swam, swum* Also called apophony or vowel gradation. Ablaut pertains to the *synchronic shifting or "grading" of vowels, but the term is also used to speak of *diachronic gradation (also called *vowel shift), which pertains to the evolution of language over time.

absolute. *adj.* Of words and clauses, standing apart grammatically from the other elements in a sentence (Lat. *absolutum,* "free from, separate").

absolute object. *See* cognate accusative.

absolute tense. *n.* The indication of *time using *tense forms.

absolute time. *n.* The signification of *time related directly to the speaker/writer's time frame, as opposed to *relative time, in which the temporal relationship is dependent on the time of the *main verb. That is, relative time means the time of the verbal action is dependent on or relative to another part of speech. Traditionally time has been thought of, generally speaking, as *absolute in the indicative mood but relative or unstated outside the indicative. *See also* absolute tense.

abstract noun. *n.* A *substantive that signifies a concept, quantity, quality or state (among other things), as in *hatred* and *sportsmanship.* It is the opposite of a *concrete noun, which refers to something tangible or real (wall, ocean, etc.).

accent. *n.* The stress placed on a syllable, or the symbol (*diacritical mark) standing above a vowel to denote that it is an emphasized syllable. In classical Greek, words were accented by a modulation of pitch, but gradually this was replaced by simply giving accented syllables greater vocal prominence (i.e., stress). The written accents were apparently introduced by grammarians who, during the growing influence of Koine Greek, wished to preserve the language as it had once been spoken. The New Testament *autographa did not contain accents; the accents were added later. Today students are usually taught

to treat all three accents—*acute, *grave and *circumflex—alike, giving accented syllables slightly more stress.

accentuation. n. The accenting of words or the accenting system of a language. See accent.

accidence. n. The study of word formation, including changes in words
due to *inflection.

accretion. n. In textual criticism, material that was added to the biblical
text (Lat. accrescere, "to grow"). The term can be used broadly to refer
to any scribal change—amendments, alterations, *glosses, corrections
and *harmonizations—whether intentional or accidental.

accusative. adj. or n. The *case that usually marks a noun, pronoun or
other substantive as the *object of the verbal action, i.e., functioning as
the *direct object.

accusative of content. See cognate accusative.

accusative of extent. n. An accusative case substantive that delimits the
extent of the verbal action in terms of how far or how long. E.g.,
ἀπεσπάσθη ἀπ᾽ αὐτῶν ὡσεὶ λίθου βολήν ("he withdrew from them
about a stone's throw," Lk 22:41); also Acts 20:16; John 2:12.

accusative of extent of space. See accusative of extent.

accusative of extent of time. See accusative of extent.

accusative of general reference. n. The subject of the *infinitive, which
appears in the accusative. E.g., ποιήσατε τοὺς ἀνθρώπους ἀναπεσεῖν
("Make the people sit down," Jn 6:10); also Acts 7:19; 11:15; 1 Thessalonians 5:27. This term may also be used to refer to the *accusative of
respect.

accusative of manner. See adverbial accusative.

accusative of measure. See accusative of extent.

accusative of reference. See accusative of respect.

accusative of respect. n. An accusative case substantive that indicates
what the verbal action is referring to. E.g., τοὔνομα ("with respect to
name," Mt 27:57); also Romans 10:5; Ephesians 4:15; Revelation 1:20.

accusative of retained object. n. An accusative case substantive that in an
*object complement construction with an *active verb retains its case
when the verb is *passive. See Luke 7:29; 1 Corinthians 12:13.

accusativum pendens. Lat. "hanging accusative." See pendent accusative.

active. adj. or n. The *voice that signifies that the *subject is performing
or causing the verbal action.

acute accent. n. An *accent that appears as a forward slanting mark above
vowels (ά) and was originally used to signify a rise in pitch (Lat. "sharp").

ad sensum. See constructio ad sensum.

adiaphora. *n.* In theology and ethics, matters not essential to the Christian faith.

adjectival. *adj.* Functioning in some way like an *adjective.

adjective. *n.* A word that modifies or qualifies a *substantive or describes a state or quality.

adjective genitive. *See* descriptive genitive.

adjunct. *n.* A *modifying word or phrase that functions in an auxiliary capacity; it can be omitted without rendering the sentence *ungrammatical.

adjunctive. *adj.* Denoting an addition with the sense of "also." The adjunctive use of καί carries this meaning, in which it functions as an *adverb.

adnominal. *adj.* Of words and phrases, modifying a *noun. —*n.* A word or phrase that modifies a noun.

adverb. *n.* A word that modifies a verb, adjective or another adverb (Lat. "toward the verb").

adverbial. *adj.* Functioning in some way like an *adverb. The term is used to describe *infinitives, *participles, *prepositional phrases or *clauses generally whose function is to *modify a *verb or make an assertion related to the *main verb.

adverbial accusative. *n.* An accusative case substantive that modifies the verbal action. Normally categorized under more restrictive headings, such as manner, extent, etc. (e.g., accusative of extent). See Matthew 6:33; Galatians 2:21.

adverbial clause. *n.* A *dependent clause functioning adverbially. Adverbial clauses convey things like cause, concession, condition, place, purpose, reason, result and time.

adverbial dative. *See* dative of manner.

adverbial participle. *n.* A participle that modifies and is subordinate to another verb. Adverbial participles are often categorized under more restrictive headings, such as temporal, purpose, means, etc. Also called the circumstantial or conjunctive participle.

adverbial preposition. *See* improper preposition.

adversative. *adj.* Denoting contrast or opposition. —*n.* A *conjunction (e.g., ἀλλά) carrying this sense (Lat. *adversari*, "to oppose").

aetiologia. *n.* In rhetoric, providing a reason to a main argument. See Romans 1:16.

affective meaning. *See* connotation.

affix. *n.* An element added to a word, *stem or *root, such as a *prefix (added to the beginning of a word), a *suffix (added to the end of a word) or an *infix (added in the middle of a word).

affliction list. *See* hardship list.

affricate. *n.* A sound produced by a *stop closure followed immediately by a slow release (a *fricative or spirant), which is characteristic of a fricative. E.g., the "j" and "ch" sound; in Greek the sounds produced by ζ, ψ and χ.

agent. *n.* The doer or instigator of the verbal action. In Greek there are three levels of agency: primary (also called ultimate or personal), secondary (or intermediate) and *instrumental/impersonal.

agentive. *adj.* Denoting the *agent of the verbal action.

agentless. *adj.* Lacking an explicitly named *agent, as in the sentence "Lori was given the key to the city."

aggadah. *See* haggadah.

agglutination. *n.* The stringing together of word elements to form words (often these *morphemes retain their original sense). *Compound words are the result of agglutination.

agglutinative language. *n.* A language in which words are generally formed by stringing together different word elements.

agrapha. Plural of *agraphon.

agraphon. *n.* A *noncanonical saying attributed to Jesus (neuter singular form of ἀγραφος, "unwritten"). See Acts 20:35. *pl.* agrapha.

agreement. *n.* The grammatical feature of language that requires certain words to correspond in *form to other related words. Also called *concord.

aitiologia. *n.* In rhetoric, a *dialogue with an imaginary partner, involving questions and answers. See Romans 9:19-20. *See also* diatribe.

Aktionsart. *n.* The feature of the Greek language whereby the quasi-objective quality of the verbal action is indicated (duration, repetition, momentary occurrence, etc.), both morphologically by *tense forms and lexico-syntactically according to contextual features. Some older grammars used the term synonymously with *aspect. *pl. Aktionsarten.*

Alexandrian Text. *See* Alexandrian text-type.

Alexandrian text-type. *n.* One of several *text-types thought to be traceable to Alexandria, Egypt, and regarded very highly by most scholars. Some have differentiated a text-type called the "neutral text," which is closely related to the Alexandrian and most likely a more primitive form of it (i.e., proto-Alexandrian). Also referred to as the Egyptian, Hesychian or Beta text-type.

Alexandrinus. *See* Codex Alexandrinus.

allegory. *n.* A narrative in which characters, objects and events serve as symbols of other things (ἀλληγορέω, "speak in another way"). Allegory is symbolic representation; it is in effect an extended *metaphor.

alliteration. *n.* The occurrence of two or more words having the same initial letter or sound (Lat. *littera*, "letter").

allomorph. *n.* A variant phonetic form of a *morpheme.

allophone. *n.* A variant form of a *phoneme.

allusion. *n.* An indirect, imprecise or passing reference in which verbal correspondence to the source text is relatively remote. A *citation or quotation, on the other hand, contains a portion of the source text that is obvious and normally relatively longer. Also called an echo.

allusive plural. *See* generalizing plural.

alpha privative. *n.* A prefixed alpha that makes a word *negative. English has *privatives that are similar to Greek, including a-, non- and un-.

Alpha Text. *See* Byzantine text-type.

alveolar. *n.* A sound produced by raising the tongue to the alveolar ridge (the sloped ridge behind the front teeth).

amalgamation. *n.* The coalescing of two consonants to form a third. For example, when κ, γ and ξ come into contact with σ, they amalgamate to form ξ.

amanuensis. *n.* A person who takes dictation, a secretary (Lat. "by hand"). The difference in *style between New Testament letters that are signed by the same person (e.g., 1 and 2 Pet) is sometimes accounted for by the use of an amanuensis who would have been given a degree of freedom in the writing process. See Romans 16:22; 1 Peter 5:12.

anachronism. *n.* A chronological error in which someone or something is misplaced in time.

anacoenosis. *n.* In rhetoric, a request for advice about a course of action. See Philippians 1:22-24. *See also* aporia.

anacoluthon. *n.* A departure from the original *grammatical construction of a sentence; a change from one type of *construction to another, rendering the sentence *ungrammatical (ἀνακόλουθον, "inconsistent"); a grammatical non sequitur. See 2 Peter 1:17-18.

anadiplosis. *n.* The repetition of a word (or group of words) at the end of one clause and the beginning of the next clause. *See also* climax. See Romans 8:17.

analogic change. *n.* A change in language in which a rule is generalized to apply to *forms hitherto unaffected (e.g., "funner" as the *comparative form of *fun*). Also referred to as internal borrowing.

analytical lexicon. *n.* A book that provides lists of words in their various inflected *forms (*see* inflection), along with parsing information and definitions. Similar to a *parsing guide.

anaphor. *n.* In linguistics, a substantive (usually a pronoun) that always has an *antecedent, such as *reflexive and *reciprocal pronouns. The opposite of cataphor (whose reference is forward).

anaphora. *n.* A reference back to a previous context by the repetition or the inclusion of a word or phrase (ἀναφορά, "a carrying back"). The anaphoric article, for example, points back to something stated or implied in a previous context. In rhetoric, anaphora occurs when successive clauses begin with the same word or group of words. See Romans 3:22, 24-25. Also known as epanadiplosis and epanaphora. The opposite of anaphora is cataphora, in which the reference is forward.

anaphoric. *adj.* Referring back. *See also* anaphora.

anaptotic. *adj.* Of languages, tending to become uninflected (*see* inflection, inflected language) over time.

anaptyctic. *adj.* Relating to *anaptyxis, the insertion of a vowel. It can also be used to describe vowels when they change over time (i.e., *vowel shift).

anaptyxis. *n.* *Epenthesis (insertion) of a vowel.

anarthrous. *adj.* Lacking the *article (ἀν, *privative + ἄρθρον, "joint"). It is the opposite of *arthrous.

anastrophe. *n.* An inversion of normal word order for *emphasis, as in "Handsome was he." See 1 Corinthians 7:27.

anathema. *n.* Curses or words of denunciation, or that which is cursed. The word is a *transliteration of ἀνάθεμα. See Galatians 1:9.

annominatio. *n.* The use of words that sound alike and have the same sense. See Matthew 16:18; Acts 8:30; Romans 12:3; 2 Thessalonians 3:11.

antanaclasis. *n.* Repetition of the same word with a different or opposite sense. E.g., νόμος in Romans 7.

antecedent. *adj.* or *n.* The word that a *pronoun is replacing or pointing back to (Lat. *ante*, "before" + *cedere*, "to go"). In the sentence "The music has begun, and it is lovely," the pronoun *it* finds its antecedent in *music*.

antecedent action. *n.* Action that occurs prior to other action. Some grammars advise treating aorist participles as indicating antecedent action. This is a good general rule, but there are many exceptions.

antepenult. *n.* The third *syllable from the end of a word, followed by the penult (next-to-last) and ultima (last). Also called antepenultima.

antepenultima. *See* antepenult.

anthropomorphism. *n.* The ascribing of human characteristics to God.

anthropopathism. *n.* The ascribing of human emotions to God. Also called anthropopathy.

antilegomena. *pl. n.* Old and New Testament books whose inspiration and canonicity (*see* canon) were disputed (ἀντιλεγόμενος, "spoken against"), as opposed to those that were accepted by all (i.e., *homologoumena). In the New Testament, the books of Hebrews, 2 Peter, James, Jude, 2 and 3 John, and Revelation.

antimetabole. *n.* In rhetoric, a statement along with a repetition of the same words in reverse order or with different grammatical functions. See Mark 2:27; Galatians 2:20.

Antiochene text-type. *See* Byzantine text-type.

antiphrasis. *n.* The use of a word in a sense opposite to its normal meaning (ἀντιφράζειν, "to express by the opposite"). E.g., 1 Corinthians 4:8, 10. *See also* irony.

antiptosis. *n.* A shifting of the normal word order that results in a change in *case. E.g., σε in Mark 1:24 is really the *predicate nominative of τίς εἶ. *See also* prolepsis.

antistrophe. *n.* The repetition of a word or *phrase at the end of two or more successive *clauses or *stanzas. See 1 Corinthians 1:25; 9:20; 13:11. Also called epiphora and epistrophe.

antithesis. *n.* In rhetoric, the use of contrast for rhetorical effect (ἀντίθεσις, "a placing in opposition"). See 1 Corinthians 1:25-29.

antonomasia. *n.* Substitution of one name for another (ἀντονομασία, "a naming instead"): either a title for a proper name (e.g., "Mr. President"); or a well-known name for a person or place (e.g., "the New York City of Asia," "Marcus is the local Casanova"). See Romans 5:14.

antonym. *n.* A word that is the opposite of another term.

aorist. *adj.* or *n.* The tense that usually presents the verbal action simply and in summary fashion. This is in contrast to the notion commonly conveyed by the imperfect: ongoing action. In the indicative mood, the aorist commonly denotes past time. The aorist is sometimes spoken of as *indefinite.

aoristic perfect. *n.* A perfect-tense verb that vividly describes a past action. Also called the dramatic or historical perfect

aoristic present. *See* instantaneous present.

aphaeresis. *n.* The loss of an element from the beginning of a word, as in *gator* from *alligator*. Also apheresis. *See also* aphesis, apocope and elision.

aphesis. *n.* The loss of an unstressed vowel from the beginning of a word, as in *lone* from *alone*. Also called front-clipping. The opposite of *apocope.

aphorism. *n.* A terse statement expressing a truth or defining a principle (ἀφορισμός, "definition"). Sometimes used to classify sayings in the Gospels. *See also* chreia.

aphoristic future. *See* gnomic future.

Apocalypse, apocalypse. *n.* The book of Revelation (ἀποκάλυψις, "revelation"); or more generally, an *apocalyptic work.

apocalyptic. *adj.* Pertaining to prophetic disclosure (ἀποκάλυψις, "uncovering, revelation"). —*n.* An apocalyptic work. As a *genre, apocalyptic, such as the book of Revelation, is characterized by the recounting of visions, abundant symbolism and an emphasis on eschatological judgment. The social movement behind such works is called apocalypticism.

apocopation. *n. See* apocope.

apocope. *n.* The loss of an element from the end of a word, as in *goin'* from *going*. Also called apocopation or back-clipping. The opposite of *aphesis.

Apocrypha, the. *n.* The collection of Jewish writings that were included in the *Septuagint, transmitted by the early church, but ultimately excluded from the Protestant *canon of Scripture. Sometimes called the Old Testament Apocrypha or deuterocanonical books. The term is also used of early Christian writings (e.g., apocryphal *gospels) not included in the New Testament canon.

apodosis. *n.* The "then" clause of a *conditional (if-then) sentence. It tells what will happen at the fulfillment of the premise presented in the "if" clause, the *protasis (ἀπόδοσις, "the act of giving back"). See 2 Peter 2:9.

apographa. *pl. n.* Copies of an *original; specifically the copies of the *autographa made by *scribes.

Apollonian canon. *See* Apollonius's canon.

Apollonius's canon. *n.* The rule that when one noun governs another noun (i.e., they occur "in *regimen") *both* either have or lack the *article. Named after Apollonius Dyscolus, a grammarian of the second century A.D. It is usually handled in the grammars under a discussion of the *genitive since the *construction includes a *head noun and a genitive noun.

Apollonius's corollary. *n.* The rule that when one *anarthrous noun governs another anarthrous noun (i.e., they occur "in *regimen") both will normally have the same semantic force, whether *definite, *indefinite or *qualitative. It is termed a corollary because it is related to *Apollonius's canon.

apophasis. *n.* An ironic declaration of intention not to speak of something, which amounts to a disclosure of it, as in "I will not bring up the fact that Timothy owes me money." See 2 Corinthians 9:4; Philemon 19. Also called preterition. *See also* paralipsis.

apophony. *See* ablaut.

apophthegm. *See* apothegm.

aporia. *n.* In rhetoric, pretending to be indecisive, in which the speaker/ writer seeks advice and considers alternatives, none of which is entirely promising (see 2 Cor 3:1). Or this term refers to any perplexing difficulty (related to ἀπορέω, "I am at a loss") in life or in a text (e.g., a contradiction or *paradox). *See also* anacoenosis.

aposiopesis. *n.* A breaking off in midsentence or the failure to include a grammatically necessary element—thought to be due to passionate feelings on the part of the writer. It is often marked by an ellipsis (. . .) in written English (ἀποσιώπησις, "keeping silent"). See Mark 11:32; Luke 13:9; 19:42; John 6:62; Acts 23:9; Romans 7:24; 2 Corinthians 3:13. *See also* brachylogy, ellipsis.

apostrophe. *n.* In *orthography, the superscripted mark (') that indicates an omission of a letter or letters (e.g., ἀπ᾽ ἐμοῦ). In rhetoric, turning away from the audience (ἀποστροφή, "turning away") to address someone or something that cannot respond (e.g., a deceased person, a geographical location, an idea). See Romans 2:1; Galatians 3:1.

apothegm. *n.* A terse, pithy, instructive statement; a maxim; an *aphorism. In *form criticism, apothegm refers to a brief story that reaches a climactic point with a saying of Jesus. Also apophthegm. These are also called *chreia, *paradigms and *pronouncement stories.

apparatus. *See* critical apparatus.

apparatus criticus. Lat. "*critical apparatus."

appellative. *adj.* or *n.* A *common noun, as opposed to a *proper noun. Also a name or descriptive epithet.

apposition. *n.* The juxtaposition of two elements (words or phrases) with the second renaming or defining the first. Paul begins his letters with words in apposition: "Paul, apostle." Both are usually in the same *case because they have the same syntactical relation to the other parts of the sentence. Sometimes, however, the second element is in the *genitive case, as in "city of Jerusalem."

appositional. *adj.* In an appositional relationship. *See* apposition.

appositional participle. *See* redundant participle.

appositive. *adj.* Being in *apposition. —*n.* A word or phrase in apposition.

appositive genitive. *See* genitive of apposition.

Aquila. *prop. n.* A convert to Judaism who produced a Greek translation of the Old Testament around A.D. 130. Origen, in producing his *Hexapla, included Aquila's translation in one column.

Aramaic. *n.* A Semitic language, closely related to Hebrew, that was widely spoken in southwest Asia from the seventh century B.C. to the seventh century A.D. Part of the Old Testament and most of the *Talmud were written in Aramaic, and Jesus is thought to have spoken it primarily.

Aramaism. *n.* Any characteristic of *Aramaic that resonates in the Greek *style of the *Septuagint or the New Testament. The term is likewise used of texts that are supposed to have been based on an Aramaic original. See Mark 2:23-28.

archaism. *n.* The inclusion of a word or expression that reflects earlier usage or *style. Also referred to as a linguistic *anachronism.

archetype. *n.* In textual criticism, a prototypical *manuscript that assumedly stands behind the different manuscripts of a given *text-type. Archetypal manuscripts are hypothetical, since every manuscript is ultimately derived from the *autographs. In *literary studies, an image or pattern that recurs throughout literature and life.

aretalogy. *n.* A story or collection of stories of the miraculous deeds of a god or godlike hero.

arthrous. *adj.* Having the *article; *articular. It is the opposite of *anarthrous.

article. *n.* The part of speech that has the ability to identify, make *definite or conceptualize, among other things. *See also* definite article, indefinite article.

articular. *adj.* Having the *article. *Adjectives, *adverbs, *infinitives, *nouns, *participles, *prepositional phrases and even whole *sentences can all be articular. Also referred to as arthrous (the opposite of *anarthrous).

articulatory phonetics. *n.* The study of the actual sounds of language—how they are produced by the vocal apparatus.

ascensive. *adj.* Reaching a climax.

ascensive conjunction. *n.* A conjunction used to add one last piece of information, which may be out of the ordinary or perhaps even the most important point (*ascensive means "rising"). The conjunction καί can be used this way, in which case it is usually translated "even."

aspect. *n.* The feature of the Greek language inherent to the *tense system that denotes the speaker/writer's subjective viewpoint or portrayal of the verbal action, whether progressive ("internal," "imperfective"), summary ("external," "perfective") or *perfect/*stative.

aspirate. *v.* or *n.* The phonetic designation for the "h" sound, represented in Greek by the *rough breathing mark over initial *vowels.

asseverative particle. *n.* A *particle used to heighten the solemnity of an assertion or an oath. See 1 Corinthians 15:31; Hebrews 6:14 (variant reading).

assimilation. *n.* One consonant becoming more like an adjacent consonant, assuming some of its qualities (Lat. *assimilo*, "I make similar"). *See also* progressive and regressive assimilation. In *textual criticism, assimilation refers to the coalescence of two *readings, either variant readings or distinct texts, usually in the Gospels. *See also* conflation.

associative dative. *See* dative of association.

assonance. *n.* Similarity of sounds between syllables or words. *See also* alliteration, paronomasia.

asyndetic. *adj.* Unconnected. The term is used of a style of writing that lacks *conjunctions (i.e., *asyndeton). *See also* parataxis.

asyndeton. *n.* The absence of *conjunctions linking coordinate words or phrases (ἀσύνδετον, "not bound together"). See Mark 2:11; Romans 1:29-31. *See also* parataxis.

athematic conjugation. *n.* The group of verbs that *decline similarly because their *inflections are not being controlled by the presence of a thematic vowel (*see* connecting vowel). This group of verbs is also referred to as the μι *conjugation (or μι verbs) since -μι is a typical *ending.

athematic verb. *See* athematic conjugation.

attendant circumstance. *n.* A function of participles, clauses or even prepositions, it refers to an action that is somewhat independent of (or perhaps coordinate with) the main action of a sentence.

attenuation. *n.* Of vowels, weakening or "thinning" in value or duration.

Attic Greek. *n.* A *dialect of ancient Greek that assumed a prominent place in writing and is sometimes used synonymously with "classical Greek." The Greek of the New Testament, *Koine, traces its heritage to Attic.

Atticism. *n.* A resorting to the classic *Attic Greek style, which became fashionable during the *Hellenistic period. Also called *classicism.

attitude. *n.* A semantic category *grammaticalized by the verb *mood forms, in which the speaker/writer presents his or her conception of an action's relationship to reality.

attraction. *n.* The transfer of the *case of an *antecedent to a *relative pronoun. Relative pronouns normally take the *gender and *number of their antecedent, while their case is determined by their function in their *relative clauses. Thus very often relative pronouns and their antecedents do not share the same case. Their close connection, however, explains why sometimes they react to one another. When attraction occurs, the relative pronoun is influenced by the antecedent and takes on its case (e.g., Jn 4:14). The reverse (*inverse attraction) can also occur, but it is more rare.

attributed genitive. *n.* A genitive substantive whose governing noun functions in some sense as an *attributive adjective, as in καινότητι ζωῆς ("newness of life," Rom 6:4). Also called the reverse genitive. See Philippians 1:22; 1 Peter 1:7.

attribution. *n.* The occurrence of attributing or describing.

attributive. *adj.* *Adjectival. (For the syntactical structure *see* attributive position.)

attributive adjective. *n.* An adjective that directly modifies a *substantive.

attributive genitive. *n.* A genitive that makes an *attribution about a *substantive. It appears where one might expect an adjective and thus it can be readily translated into one, as in "body of sin" (σῶμα τῆς ἁμαρτίας), which means "sinful body" (Rom 6:6). Its frequency in the New Testament is due to Semitic influence on New Testament Greek (*see* Semitism); thus it is sometimes referred to as the Hebrew genitive. Also called the genitive of quality.

attributive position. *n.* A construction in which an adjective or participle is immediately preceded by the article; thus it functions to attribute a quality to a noun. *See also* first, second and third attributive position.

augment. *n.* In the indicative mood, a *prefix added to a verbal form (in the imperfect, aorist or pluperfect) to indicate past *time. This is achieved either by adding a vowel if the word begins with a consonant, or by *lengthening the *opening vowel (ε becomes η; o becomes ω).

augmentation. *n.* In the indicative mood, the adding of a vowel to the front of a word to indicate past *time. If the word already begins with a vowel, the vowel is *lengthened (ε becomes η; o becomes ω).

Augustinian hypothesis. *n.* Augustine's solution to the *synoptic problem, in which he suggested that Matthew was written first; then Mark, depending on Matthew, was written second; then Luke, depending on both Matthew and Mark, was written third.

authorial intent(ion). *n.* In biblical interpretation, the perceived aim of the author. For some, recovering the author's intention in a text is the goal of interpretation. It *is* interpretation. However, to what extent the interpreter must be concerned about the original intention of the author is a matter of debate. *See also* reader-response criticism, *sensus plenior.*

autograph. *n.* An *original handwritten document (αὐτόγραφος, "written in one's own hand").

autographa. Plural of *autograph.

auxiliary verb. *n.* A verb that appears alongside another *verbal form to "help" portray a certain type of action (they are referred to as helping verbs). The use of auxiliary verbs is more common in English, but an example in Greek is the *periphrastic construction, a form of εἰμί and a *participle.

B

Babylonian Talmud. *n.* The *Mishnah plus the Babylonian *Gemara (commentary).

back. *adj.* Of speech sounds, articulated in the back of the mouth or with the back of the tongue.

back translation. *n.* The process or result of translating not from the *source language to the *target language but the other way around. Thus some scholars have attempted to "back translate" from the Greek of the Gospels to an underlying Aramaic *Urtext.

back-clipping. *See* apocope.

backgrounding. *v.* or *n.* The giving of remoteness or deemphasis to a linguistic element. *See also* foregrounding.

barytone. *n.* A word whose final syllable is unaccented. *See also* oxytone, paroxytone and proparoxytone.

base. Another term for *stem.

Behnesa. *See* Oxyrhynchus papyri.

Benedictus. *n.* The name given to Zacharias's hymn about John the Baptist in Luke 1:68-79, derived from the opening words in the *Vulgate: *Benedictus Dominus,* "Praise be to the Lord."

benefactive middle. *See* indirect middle.

Beta Text. *See* Alexandrian text-type.

Bezae. *See* Codex Bezae.

biblical criticism. *n.* The study of Scripture using the canons of science and reason according to prescribed methods (e.g., *textual criticism, *historical criticism, *form criticism, *tradition criticism, *redaction criticism, *literary criticism). The term is used generally with reference to any or all of these interrelated disciplines.

biblical Greek. *n.* The type of Greek as it appears in the New Testament and the *Septuagint. The term was coined with the idea in mind (since proved false) that it was a peculiar *dialect. With the discovery of a great number of Greek papyri (private letters, accounts, wills, reports, etc.), it became evident that the New Testament was simply written in the first-century *vernacular. *See* Koine.

bicolon. *n.* Two cola (lines of text written according to the number of *syllables). *See* colon. Also bicola.

bilabial. *adj.* or *n.* A speech sound produced by bringing the lips together.

Bildhälfte. Germ. "picture half." —*n.* The part of a *parable that pertains to the imagery or mental picture, as opposed to the meaningful content or "reality" (*Sachhälfte*).

blend(ing). *n.* A word composed of the parts of more than one word (e.g., "brunch," breakfast + lunch; "smog," smoke + fog). In grammar, blending involves the combining of two elements that do not normally occur together, which form a single linguistic unit. —*v.* To combine elements in this manner.

borrowing. *n.* The appropriation of words from one language into another. *See also* loanword.

bound form. *See* bound morpheme.

bound morpheme. *n.* A meaningful speech unit (*morpheme) that is not used independently but attaches to other *forms (e.g., *alpha privative).

brachylogy. *n.* Condensed, abbreviated speech or writing, usually involving the omission of an element of language that must be supplied from the context to fully complete the meaning (βραχυλογία, "short speech"). Grammars often do not differentiate between brachylogy and *ellipsis. *See also* aposiopesis.

bracketing. *See* inclusio.

breathing mark. *n.* A diacritical mark standing above word-initial vowels (or diphthongs), indicating whether the vowel sound is *aspirated or not. Greek has two breathing marks: the *rough breathing mark (ἁ), which signals aspiration, and the *smooth breathing mark (ἀ), which indicates its absence.

brevior lectio potior. Lat. "the *shorter reading is preferable."

brevior lectio probabilior. Lat. "the *shorter reading is more probable."

broadening. *n.* A semantic change in which the meaning of a word becomes more extensive over time. The opposite of *narrowing.

Byzantine Text. *See* Byzantine text-type.

Byzantine text-type. *n.* One of several *text-types, disseminated throughout the Byzantine Empire and discernible in the majority of *extant *manuscripts (thus it is often referred to as the Majority Text). This text provided the basis for Erasmus's edition of the Greek New Testament, the *Textus Receptus and the King James Version. Also called the Alpha, Antiochene, Koine, Lucianic or Syrian text.

C

Caesarean text-type. *n.* A proposed *text-type thought to be traceable to Caesarea. It has close affinities to the Alexandrian and Western texts. Many scholars do not consider it sufficiently distinct to be thought of as a separate text-type.

calling story. *n.* In the Gospels, a story in which Jesus calls a person to obey or follow him.

canon. *n.* The collection of writings accepted as inspired and therefore authoritative; the Bible. In textual criticism, a dictum or rule that is used as a guide in trying to determine which *reading among the various *witnesses is the original.

Canon of Apollonius. *See* Apollonius's canon.

canonical. *adj.* Pertaining to the biblical *canon, the accepted collection of books that form the Bible. For example, to follow the canonical order means one follows a sequence based on the arrangement of the books of the Bible, as opposed to chronological order.

canonical criticism. *n.* Interpretation of the biblical text that deliberately operates from the standpoint of an accepted *canon or focuses on texts in their *canonical framework, including how a book's inclusion and placement in the canon affects interpretation. Canonical criticism began as a protest of methods that were thought to be reductionistic or preoccupied with matters of authenticity. Yet the term can also encompass these same concerns (i.e., authorship, inspiration, *pseudonymity, tradition).

canons of criticism. *pl. n.* In textual criticism, criteria for determining the *originality of *variant readings in the textual tradition.

capitulation. *See* kephalaia.

captatio benevolentiae. *n.* A conventional stylistic feature of speeches and letters in which the speaker/writer begins with complimentary words (Lat. "capture of good will"). See Acts 24:2-4, 10; 26:2-3.

Captivity Epistles. *See* Prison Epistles.

cardinal number. *n.* A number used to indicate quantity, either in counting (1, 2, 3, etc.) or when the number functions like an *adjective ("twelve disciples"). This is in contrast to *ordinal numbers, which indicate order or position (first, second, third, etc.).

Carmen Christi. Lat. "Hymn of Christ." —*n.* Designation for Philippians 2:6-11, thought by some scholars to be an early Christian, pre-Pauline confession or hymn. This term is sometimes used of other "Christ hymns" reputed to be embedded in the New Testament (e.g., Col 1:15-20). *See also carmina.*

carmina. Lat. "hymns."—*pl. n.* Used of biblical texts that might contain or derive from earlier *hymnic material (Phil 2:6-11; Col 1:15-20). *See also Carmen Christi.*

case. *n.* The feature of language that indicates the syntactical function of nouns, pronouns, adjectives and participles. In Greek and other *inflected languages, this is achieved by means of declensional *endings. *See also* five-case and eight-case system.

case ending. *n.* A word-final morpheme that marks a word's *case. Case endings are obviously used only with words that have case: nouns, pronouns, adjectives and participles. *Personal endings, on the other hand, are used with verbs to indicate person and number. Case endings are also referred to as terminations or case terminations.

casus instrumentalis. Lat. "*instrumental case" (according to the *eight-case system).

casus pendens. Lat. "hanging case." —*n.* This term is used most often of the *nominative absolute, especially the *pendent nominative, which is thought of as suspended or "hanging" apart from its clause.

catachresis. *n.* A misuse or strained use of language; or the use of an improper *form of a word.

cataphor. *See* anaphor, anaphora.

categoric(al) plural. *See* generalizing plural.

catena. *n.* A series of words, phrases, verses, quotations or stories linked together (Lat. "chain"). The term may refer in a more specialized sense to compiled excerpts of patristic *commentary (a catena commentary), usually printed along with the biblical text to more fully explicate its meaning. *See also* florilegium. *pl.* catenae.

catenative construction. *See* complementary infinitive.

Catholic Epistles. *n.* A designation for James; 1 and 2 Peter; 1, 2 and 3 John; and Jude, which were thought to be addressed to no particular church but generally to the church at large.

causal clause. *n.* An *adverbial clause denoting cause, reason or basis.

causal infinitive. *n.* An infinitive used in a *dependent clause that indicates cause, reason or basis. Causal infinitives almost always appear in the idiomatic construction διὰ + τό + infinitive. See Luke 2:4; 11:8; Philippians 1:7.

causal participle. *n.* A participle that denotes cause, reason or basis.

causative active. *n.* The use of the *active voice to indicate that the *subject is the indirect cause of the verbal action. Also known as the ergative active voice.

causative middle. *n.* The use of the *middle voice to indicate that the *subject has something done to or for itself.

causative verb. *n.* A verb denoting causation. *Transitive verbs are causative, but occasionally a causative sense is given to intransitive verbs so that they have an *object. *See* transitive, intransitive.

cause infinitive. *See* causal infinitive.

cause participle. *See* causal participle.

cento. *n.* A patchwork of biblical quotations. See Romans 3:10-18; 11:34-35; 1 Peter 2:6-8; Hebrews 1:5-13; 8:8-12. The term can also refer to a *literary work that was produced by blending various sources (Lat. "patched cloth"). *pl.* centos.

chain-saying. *n.* Any expression that consists of a succession of linked *clauses. See 1 Peter 1:6-7. *See also* climax, *Stichwort*.

chiasm. *n.* A literary device in which words, clauses or themes are laid out and then repeated but in inverted order. This creates an a-b-b-a pattern, or a "crossing" effect like the letter "x" (χιασμός, "a making of the letter χ"). Also called inverted parallelism. See Romans 10:9-10; 1 Corinthians 1:24-25; Ephesians 5:5; Philemon 5.

chiasmus. Lat. "*chiasm."

chreia. *n.* In ancient rhetoric, a literary form containing a concise, pointed saying attributed to a well-known person and useful for daily living (χρεία). Some chreiai are simple sayings; others recount a person's deeds at greater length. The term is used in *form criticism of pointed sayings of Jesus. Also spelled chria. *pl.* chriae. *See also* apothegm, pronouncement story.

chrestomathy. *n.* A compilation of selected literary passages to aid in language learning.

Christian canon. *See* canon.

circumflex accent. *n.* The *accent that appears as a curved line above vowels (e.g., σῶμα) and was originally used to signify a rising and falling pitch (Lat. *circumflexus,* "bending around").

circumlocution. *n.* A roundabout way of saying something (Lat. *circumlocutio,* "roundabout speech"). Can be synonymous with *periphrasis.

circumstantial participle. *n.* A participle that modifies another verb. Circumstantial participles are usually categorized under more restrictive headings, such as temporal, purpose, means, etc. Also termed *adverbial.

citation. *n.* A quotation. In contrast, an *allusion is merely a passing reference; the correspondence to the source text may be hardly noticeable.

classicism. *n.* A stylistic feature of the New Testament in which a particular *construction more closely resembles classical Greek than *Koine. These occur in Luke-Acts and Hebrews more frequently than elsewhere. Also called *Atticism.

clause. *n.* A sentence or a construction resembling a sentence that is in some sense grammatically "complete." Clauses in Greek can be either *dependent or *independent. Any clause on which other clauses are dependent is a *main clause.

climax. *n.* The arrangement of words and clauses to build suspense or create one statement more forceful or poignant than the previous one. Likewise it can refer to a crescendo or turning point in an argument or narrative. Climax also includes the repetition of a key word in a following clause, linking the clauses together to a culminating point, as in Romans 5:3-4 (κλῖμαξ, "ladder"). *See also* chain-saying.

closed vowel. *n.* A vowel sound that is pronounced with the mouth more closed than open.

closed-class words. *pl. n.* A category of words that rarely if ever has new words added to it, usually *function words such as particles and conjunctions. *See also* open-class words.

cluster. *n.* Two or more successive *consonants; or more broadly, a group of speech sounds, *morphemes, words, etc.

codex. *n.* An ancient type of book produced by folding a stack of *papyrus sheets or *vellum in half, then sewing the folded end to form a spine. Near the end of the first century A.D. the codex first appeared and eventually replaced the scroll as the book form of choice (likely popularized by early Christian use). Also referred to as a leaf-form.

Codex Alexandrinus. *n.* A fifth-century *uncial manuscript of almost the entire Bible, representative of the *Byzantine text-type in the *Gospels (the oldest example) and the *Alexandrian text-type in Acts and the *Epistles. This *codex includes one of the best texts of the book of Revelation. Represented by the *siglum "A."

Codex Bezae. *n.* A fifth- or sixth-century bilingual (Greek-Latin) *manuscript of the Gospels and Acts, constituting the principal representative of the *Western text-type. Represented by the *siglum "D." Also known as Codex Cantabrigiensis.

Codex Ephraemi. *n.* A fifth-century *palimpsest containing a little more than half the New Testament in all the major *text-types. Represented by the *siglum "C."

Codex Sinaiticus. *n.* A fourth-century *vellum *uncial manuscript containing the entire New Testament and most of the Old Testament, exemplifying the *Alexandrian text-type mainly. Represented by the Hebrew letter aleph (א).

Codex Vaticanus. *n.* A fourth-century *vellum manuscript of almost the entire Bible, exemplifying the *Alexandrian text-type. Represented by the *siglum "B."

Codex Washington. *n.* A late fourth- or early fifth-century *manuscript of the Gospels, exemplifying a variety of *text-types. Represented by the *siglum "W."

codices. *pl. n.* Plural of *codex.

cognate. *adj.* Of etymologically related words, sharing the same *root. — *n.* A cognate word. (Also used of related languages.) Also referred to as word sets. *See also* cognate accusative and dative.

cognate accusative. *n.* An accusative noun used alongside a verbal *cognate, as in "*fight* the good *fight*," in 1 Timothy 6:12. Also referred to as the absolute object, the accusative of inner object, accusative of content, *figura etymologica,* or *schema etymologicum.*

cognate dative. *n.* A dative noun used alongside a verbal *cognate, as in "your old men shall *dream dreams*," in Acts 2:17. Also called the internal dative.

cognitive meaning. *See* denotation.

cohortative. *See* hortatory subjunctive.

cohortative subjunctive. *See* hortatory subjunctive.

coinage. *n.* The formation and addition of new words to the *lexicon.

collate. *v.* In textual criticism, to attempt reconstruction of the original biblical text by comparing and compiling *variant readings in ancient handwritten manuscripts.

collective noun. *n.* A noun that denotes a collection of persons or things that are considered a unit.

collocation. *n.* A standard combination of words. For example, the adjective *extenuating* very regularly collocates with *circumstances*.

colloquial. *adj.* Characteristic of informal speech—the way people actually communicate day to day.

colometric. *adj.* Arranged according to cola. Colometry is evident in *Codex Bezae. *See* colon.

colon. *n.* In some ancient biblical manuscripts (e.g., *Codex Bezae [D]), a line of text containing a single clause of nine to sixteen syllables. Manuscripts were written colometrically to facilitate public readings. *pl.* cola.

colophon. *n.* A note at the end of a book giving facts about its publication, such as the date or place of writing, or about the *scribe's own personal involvement in producing it (κολοφών, "finish, end").

Colwell's rule. *n.* A dictum stating that *definite *predicate nominatives that precede the verb usually lack the article. The rule was published in 1933 by E. C. Colwell. A complement to this rule arose later (and has been erroneously thought to be the actual rule) that states an *anarthrous predicate nominative that precedes the verb is usually definite.

comitative dative. *See* dative of association.

comma. *n.* In textual criticism, a line of text that does not exceed eight *syllables. *pl.* commata.

Comma Johanneum. *See* Johannine comma.

command future indicative. *See* imperatival future.

comment. *n.* The part of a sentence that says something about the *topic or *subject. Also known as the *predicate.

commentary. *n.* A book that discusses the biblical text. There are numerous types of commentaries; they can be homiletical/theological, critical, popular, historical, sociorhetorical and so forth.

commodi. Lat. "advantage." *See* dative of advantage.

common gender. *n.* The lack of masculine-, feminine- and neuter-specific *inflections to mark *gender.

common noun. *n.* A noun that refers to one or all of the members of a class generally (e.g., pacifier, book), as opposed to a *proper noun, which refers to a particular thing (Indian Ocean, *Paradise Lost*).

common-sense criticism. *See* phenomenological criticism.

comparative. *adj.* Of adjectives and adverbs, denoting comparison. The adjective *bigger* is a comparative adjective; *big* is *positive; *biggest* is *superlative. Sometimes referred to as the comparative degree.

comparative degree. *See* comparative.

comparative for elative. *n.* The use of a *comparative adjective with the sense of an *elative. See Acts 13:31; 2 Corinthians 8:17.

comparative for superlative. *n.* The use of a *comparative adjective with the sense of a *superlative, as in Luke 9:48: "the least [lit. "smaller"] among you is greatest."

comparative genitive. *See* genitive of comparison.

comparative linguistics. *See* philology.

comparative philology. *See* philology.

comparative religion. *See* religio-historical criticism.

compensatory lengthening. *n.* In word formation, the *lengthening of a vowel to compensate for one or more letters dropping out.

complement. *n.* A grammatical element that completes the meaning of (or complements) a *predicate. —*v.* To supplement or complete the meaning of another element.

complementary distribution. *n.* The phenomenon of certain speech sounds never occurring in the same phonetic environment.

complementary infinitive. *n.* An infinitive used along with an indicative verb to complete the idea or action of the verb. Also referred to as the catenative construction. See Matthew 2:13; 1 Timothy 2:12.

complementary participle. *n.* A participle that appears in conjunction with another verb and *complements it. See Matthew 11:1; Acts 12:16; Ephesians 1:16. Sometimes referred to as the supplementary participle.

completive. *n.* An element that completes another element. For example, objects of prepositions are completives.

complex sentence. *See* compound sentence.

complexive aorist. *See* constative aorist.

composite. *adj.* or *n.* Of a text, composed from discrete sources.

composition(al) criticism. *See* redaction criticism.

compound consonant. *n.* A double *consonant.

compound sentence. *n.* A sentence consisting of two or more main *clauses. E.g., "I am the true vine, and my father is the vinedresser" (Jn 15:1).

compound verb. *n.* A verb formed by two elements: the verbal *stem and a prefixed *preposition. Sometimes the preposition will retain its meaning; at other times the preposition serves as an intensifier of the original verbal idea.

compound word. *n.* A word formed by two or more words fused together.

comprehensive aorist. *See* constative aorist.

conative. *adj.* Denoting verbal action that is intended, attempted or about to occur (Lat. *conari*, "to try"). Sometimes the inchoative is also treated alongside the conative as action that is begun but interrupted. Also called tendential or *voluntative. *See also* voluntative present.

concatenation. *n.* The linking together of words (Lat. *com*, "together" + *catenare*, "to bind"). The term is sometimes used to discuss *genitive chains.

concatenative genitives. *See* genitive chain.

concession participle. *See* concessive participle.

concessive participle. *n.* An *adverbial participle that presents action that would seemingly work against the verbal action of the main clause but does not. In other words, the action of the *main verb occurs despite the action of the participle. E.g., "Though you have not seen him, you love him" (1 Pet 1:8).

concord. *n.* The grammatical feature of a language that requires that certain words correspond in *form to other related words. For example, there is normally concord between a verb and its subject (they share person and number). Also called *agreement. The lack of concord is *discord.

concordance. *n.* An alphabetical index of all or part of the words in a work that is the focus of study (e.g., the English Bible, Greek New Testament, Josephus's works).

concrete noun. *n.* A word that signifies something material, tangible and real, as opposed to something abstract and theoretical (e.g., *man* vs. *manliness*). The contrasting terms *concrete* and *abstract* are used to classify *nouns. *See also* abstract noun.

condition participle. *n.* An *adverbial participle that indicates a condition upon which the action of the *main clause is dependent. Supplying the word *if* usually brings across the sense of the condition participle. See Matthew 21:22; Galatians 6:9.

conditional indicative. *n.* The use of an *indicative mood verb in a *first class condition or *second class condition.

conditional sentence. *n.* A sentence that presents two situations, one conditioned on the other. The "if" clause in a conditional sentence is called the *protasis; the "then" clause is called the *apodosis. Greek uses certain *structure markers or *function words to denote different types of conditional sentences. *See also* first, second, third and fourth class condition.

conditional subjunctive. *n.* The use of a subjunctive mood verb in a *third class condition.

conflate. *v.* To combine two or more elements into one whole. In textual criticism, it refers to the blending of two texts or two *variant readings.

conflate reading. *See* conflation.

conflation. *n.* The fusing together of two elements. The term is used of word formation, as well as to speak of variant texts that were combined in *transmission (i.e., expanded texts), often due to a scribe's unwillingness to choose between variants. Sometimes the term is used synonymously with *assimilation, the merging of two distinct passages (usually in the Gospels).

conflict dialogue/story. *See* controversy dialogue.

conjectural emendation. *n.* A suggestion for the wording of a particular problematic passage that is not supported by any *extant *manuscript evidence but seems nevertheless to be the best estimation as to the *original text.

conjecture. *See* conjectural emendation.

conjugate. *v.* To give the inflected *forms of a word, especially a *verb. *See* parse.

conjugation. *n.* The inflectional pattern of a word (especially verbs); or, likewise, a class of verbs with similarly inflected *forms. The term can also refer to the presentation of such a set of words in a table or a list.

conjunction. *n.* A word that functions to connect words and constructions (Lat. *conjunctus*, "joining together"). Conjunctions are normally divided into two groups: coordinating conjunctions and subordinating conjunctions. The latter are sometimes referred to as *particles. Also referred to as conjunctive.

conjunctive. *See* conjunction.

conjunctive participle. *See* adverbial participle.

connecting vowel. *n.* A vowel that in inflected languages (like Greek) adheres to certain *tense stems. In Greek, it is either an epsilon or omicron that adheres to the word's *root in order to connect it to the *personal ending. Thus it appears quite often in the word's various forms and accordingly drives the inflectional pattern. Also called thematic vowel or variable vowel.

connective. *n.* A word, such as a *conjunction, that serves to connect words or groups of words (clauses, sentences, etc.).

connotation. *n.* A secondary meaning associated with or suggested by a word (Lat. "to mark with"), in contrast to its *denotation, its dictionary definition. A word can take on a certain connotation for an individual (because of past personal experience) or have an associative element that many people understand.

connotative meaning. *See* connotation.

consecutive. *adj.* Denoting result.

consecutive clause. *n.* A clause that denotes result, as in "Gail yelled so loudly *that she lost her voice.*"

consistent eclecticism. *See* rigorous eclecticism.

consonant. *n.* A speech sound produced with a degree of obstruction or closure in the throat or mouth.

consonant declension. Synonym for the *third declension.

consonantal iota. *n.* An iota that in classical Greek was a distinct character in the alphabet but fell out of use by the time of the writing of the New Testament. Nevertheless its presence is still felt; some inflectional changes (*see* inflection) seem irregular until one recognizes that an iota was a consonantal iota.

consonantal reduplication. *n.* The duplication of an initial consonant in the formation of the *perfect and *pluperfect tenses.

constative aorist. *n.* An aorist tense verb that, along with other contextual features, presents the action simply, in summary, or as a whole. Also called complexive, comprehensive, global, historical, punctiliar, simple or summary. See John 1:11; Romans 5:14; Revelation 20:4.

constructio ad sensum. Lat. "construction according to sense." —*n.* A construction that is technically *ungrammatical but is understood nevertheless.

constructio praegnans. Lat. "*pregnant construction."

construction. *n.* A group of words that are interrelated grammatically and function together to carry meaning.

consummative aorist. *n.* An aorist tense verb that denotes completed past action, with stress on the accomplishment or fulfillment of the verbal idea. Also called the culminative, ecbatic, effective, perfective or resultative aorist. See Acts 27:43.

consummative perfect. *n.* A perfect-tense verb that denotes completed past action. Likewise the consummative perfect may have a double sense, emphasizing finished past action and affirming a result felt at the time of speaking/writing. Also referred to as the pure or extensive perfect, or the perfect of completed past action. See John 1:34.

content genitive. *See* genitive of content.

content word. *n.* A word that has identifiable *lexical meaning, as opposed to a *function word, which primarily expresses grammatical relationships.

contextual method. *n.* A method of interpreting a text by first establishing its social and historical milieu, which then helps to explain the text's meaning.

continuant. *n.* A speech sound in which the airstream continues without complete interruption. In Greek, θ, λ, μ, ν, σ, φ and ξ (as well as gamma nasal and the rough breathing).

continuative. *adj.* Denoting continuation. Sometimes used synonymously with transitional.

continuous action. *n.* Verbal action that denotes continuity or that which is ongoing. Also called progressive action.

contract verb. *n.* A verb whose stem ends in a vowel and which therefore undergoes *contraction when this vowel comes into contact with the vowel of the *personal ending.

contract vowel. *n.* The final vowel of certain verb stems that, when joined to a *personal ending that begins with a vowel, contracts.

contraction. *n.* The dropping out of letters to create new forms of words; or a word formed by such a change. This is common when *stem letters and *ending letters (or *connecting vowels) coalesce, as is the case with contract verbs whose stems end in vowels. *See* elision.

contrary-to-fact condition. *See* second class condition.

controlling verb. *n.* The main verb, upon which other words are *dependent.

controversy dialogue/story. *n.* A brief narrative that contains a pronouncement of Jesus in the context of conflict with religious authorities. Also called conflict dialogue.

convention. *n.* The arbitrary but agreed upon relationship between linguistic expressions and their meanings.

coordinate clause. *n.* A clause that is parallel to another clause, as opposed to a *dependent (subordinate) clause.

coordinate conjunction. *n.* A conjunction that joins two grammatical elements that are parallel to one another and equal in function (i.e., one is not *dependent on or subordinate to the other).

Coptic. *adj.* or *n.* An extinct language that developed from ancient Egyptian, in which portions of the Bible are extant (in several Coptic dialects). The language survives today exclusively as a liturgical language of the Coptic Church.

copula. *n.* A word that connects words or clauses; or a technical term for the *intransitive verbs εἰμί, γίνομαι and sometimes ὑπάρχω, which connect *subjects and *predicates (Lat. *copula*, "link"). *See also* equative verb.

copulative. *adj.* Functioning to connect words or clauses (Lat. *copulare*, "join together"). The term can be used of verbs (*copula for short) or *conjunctions.

copyist. *n.* A person who copied the biblical text prior to the invention of the printing press. Also referred to as a *scribe.

coreferential. *adj.* Of words and constituents in a sentence, having the same reference.

coronal. *adj.* Of a class of speech sounds including *labials, *alveolars and *palatals. —*n.* A coronal sound.

coronis. *n.* A *diacritical mark (') placed over a contracted syllable to indicate that *crasis has taken place. Identical in appearance to the smooth-breathing mark.

corpus. *n.* A body of work. For example, the Pauline corpus is the collection of writings attributed to Paul.

corrector. *n.* Someone who corrects; an editor. In textual criticism, the term signifies that the original wording of a *manuscript has been corrected one or more times (usually referred to as the first *hand, second hand, etc.).

correlative. *See* correlative conjunction.

correlative conjunction. *n.* A conjunction that occurs as one of a pair (e.g., μέν . . . δέ); together they correlate clauses that have various relationships to one another. This construction is sometimes referred to as correlative coordination.

correlative coordination. *See* correlative.

cotext. *n.* The linguistic environment of a passage; or the reflection of one text off another. The term is more precise than "context," which can refer to either linguistic or situational environments. Also co-text.

count(able) noun. *n.* A noun whose referent is thought of as separable, thus countable, so that it can be pluralized, as opposed to an uncountable or *mass noun.

crasis. *n.* The merging of two words in sequence by the omission and *contraction of vowels (κρᾶσις, "mixing"). The *breathing mark of the latter word is retained to mark the contraction. E.g., *he is* becomes *he's*; in Greek καὶ ἐγώ becomes κἀγώ; καὶ ἐμοί becomes κἀμοί.

creole or creolized language. *n.* A *pidgin language that has become the native tongue of a community.

criterion of Aramaic linguistic features. *n.* In biblical criticism, a method used to establish historically reliable Gospel material based on the presence of *Aramaisms.

criterion of coherence/consistency. *n.* In biblical criticism, a method used to establish historically reliable Gospel material based on whether it co-heres with material that was previously established as authentic.

criterion of contextual credibility. *n.* In biblical criticism, a method used to establish historically reliable Gospel material based on whether it fits into the first-century Palestinian context.

criterion of dissimilarity. *n.* In biblical criticism, a method used to establish historically reliable Gospel material based on whether it is dissimilar to contemporary Judaism or the setting of the early church. Also called the criterion of double dissimilarity. Sometimes this designation is used to describe specifically what would have worked against, or been embarrassing to, the early church. *See also* criterion of embarrassment.

criterion of divergent patterns. *n.* In biblical criticism, a method used to establish historically reliable Gospel material based on whether it is contrary to emphases of the early church.

criterion of embarrassment. *n.* In biblical criticism, a method used to establish historically reliable Gospel material based on the inclusion of information that would have been disturbing or embarrassing to the author.

criterion of independent attestation. *See* criterion of multiple attestation.

criterion of least distinctiveness. *n.* In biblical criticism, a method used to establish historically reliable Gospel material based on whether an alteration in a particular *form (e.g., the addition of detail, the *conflation of material, the elimination of *Semitisms, the preference for *direct discourse) is detected, which would signify a secondary tradition.

criterion of multiple attestation. *n.* In biblical criticism, a method used to establish historically reliable Gospel material based on whether it appears in independent strands of tradition (e.g., in Q, Mark and M). Also referred to as the criterion of independent attestation or the cross-section method.

criterion of Semitic language phenomena. *n.* In biblical criticism, a method used to establish historically reliable Gospel material based on the occurrence of *Semitisms. The term can also be used of geographical or cultural references that signify Palestinian origin for the tradition. Sometimes called the criterion of Semitisms and Palestinian background.

criterion of "unintentional" signs of history. *n.* In biblical criticism, a method used to establish historically reliable Gospel material based on whether it includes accurate details that would suggest an eyewitness account.

critical apparatus. *n.* The data presented in footnotes at the bottom of the page in a critical biblical text (*see* critical text) in which the *witnesses for the *variant readings are cited. This provides part of the rationale behind the decisions made that are reflected in the text above. Also referred to as a textual apparatus.

critical text. *n.* A printed biblical text that does not reflect any single ancient document but rather is a conjectural reconstruction and the product of *textual criticism. It is a text formed by comparing the numerous variations of the *manuscripts and including what is considered to be the superior *reading of each variation. A critical text will include a *critical apparatus.

criticism. *n.* Investigation into the origin and history of written works.

cross-pollination. *n.* The blending of characteristics of the various *text-types.

cross-pollinization. Synonymous with *cross-pollination.

crux interpretum. —*n.* A passage (often difficult to interpret) that is central to an issue or crucial to a particular doctrine (Lat. "cross [= crucial point] of interpretation").

culminative aorist. *See* consummative aorist.

cultic. *adj.* Pertaining to religious devotion expressed through established rites (e.g., the sacrificial system or the feasts).

curse optative. *n.* An *optative mood verb used specifically to wish for harm to come to someone.

cursive. *adj.* Designating a style of handwriting in which the letters are joined together, and which was employed in antiquity for everyday correspondence (letters, receipts, etc.) because it could be written rapidly (Lat. *cursus*, "run"). —*n.* This style, a letter in this style or a manuscript that is written in this style. Also referred to as *minuscule writing, a "running hand" or *scriptio continua.*

customary present. *n.* A present-tense verb that denotes action that is typical, regular, normal, continual or habitual. Used synonymously with process present and habitual or general present. See 1 Corinthians 11:26.

cynicism. *n.* A Greco-Roman philosophical school that taught that a virtuous life consisted of living independently of external forces such as social conventions and institutions, as well as the niceties of life.

D

daber halamed me °inyano. *n.* One of the rules or techniques of midrashic interpretation (*see* midrash) according to which one appeals to the larger context of a passage by merely citing a short section from it (Heb. "explanation from the context").

dative. *adj.* or *n.* The *case that is regularly used for *indirect objects, designating the person or thing to which something is given or for whom something exists or is done. It can also express the purpose or result of an action. Other uses include the dative of *advantage, *disadvantage, *possession, *manner, *cause, *reference, *place, *time, *instrument and *association.

dative of advantage. *n.* A dative case substantive that designates the person who has an interest in or benefits from the verbal action. Also referred to as the dative of interest or *dativus commodi.* E.g., ζῇ τῷ θεῷ ("he lives to God," Rom 6:10); also 2 Corinthians 5:13.

dative of agency/agent. *n.* A dative case substantive that signifies the personal *agent behind the verbal action. See Luke 23:15 (αὐτῷ); James 3:7.

dative of association. *n.* A dative case substantive that indicates someone or something with which one associates. The preposition *with* usually conveys the sense accurately. Also called the associative, comitative or sociative dative. E.g., μὴ γίνεσθε ἑτεροζυγοῦντες ἀπίστοις ("Do not be bound together with unbelievers," 2 Cor 6:14); also 2 Thessalonians 3:14.

dative of cause. *n.* A dative case substantive that indicates the cause, instrument or basis of the verbal action. See Romans 11:20, 31; Galatians 6:12.

dative of destination. *n.* A dative case substantive that denotes a goal or destination. See Matthew 21:5; Hebrews 12:22.

dative of disadvantage. *n.* A dative case substantive that designates the person who is disadvantaged or somehow negatively affected by the verbal action. Also referred to as *dativus incommodi.* E.g., μαρτυρεῖτε ἑαυτοῖς ("you bear witness against yourselves," Mt 23:31); also 1 Corinthians 11:29.

dative of feeling. *See* ethical dative.

dative of instrument/means. *n.* A dative case substantive denoting means. See John 11:2; Romans 3:28; Philippians 4:6.

dative of interest. *See* dative of advantage.

dative of manner. *n.* A dative case substantive that denotes the manner of the verbal action. Also known as the adverbial dative. See John 7:26; Philippians 1:18.

dative of place. *n.* A dative case substantive that indicates where the verbal action occurs. Also called the dative of sphere. See Matthew 5:3, 8; Acts 2:33; 5:31.

dative of possession. *n.* A dative case substantive that signifies ownership; the dative owns the *noun to which it is related. See Luke 1:14; John 1:6; Romans 7:3.

dative of reference. *n.* A *dative case *substantive that indicates what or who is being referred to in the presentation of the verbal action, or remotely affected by the verbal action. See Acts 4:36; 16:5; 1 Corinthians 14:20. Due to this latter idea, some grammars treat the dative of reference along with the dative of advantage/disadvantage, except that the notion of interest is greatly diminished. See 2 Corinthians 5:13. Also called dative of respect.

dative of respect. *See* dative of reference.

dative of sphere. *See* dative of place.

dative of time. *n.* A dative case substantive indicating when the verbal action is accomplished or for how long it occurs. See Luke 8:29; Romans 16:25; Galatians 6:9.

dativus comitativus. Lat. "comitative dative." *See* dative of association.

dativus commodi. Lat. "*dative of advantage."

dativus ethicus. Lat. "*ethical dative."

dativus incommodi. Lat. "*dative of disadvantage."

dativus relationis. Lat. "dative of relation or reference." *See* dative of reference.

dativus sociativus. Lat. "*dative of association."

daughter translation. *n.* A translation of a translation; or particularly, a translation of the *Septuagint into another language (e.g., Latin, *Coptic, Syriac), so that it is one step further removed from the original Hebrew Scriptures.

Dead Sea Scrolls. *n.* Scrolls written mostly in Hebrew and *Aramaic with a few fragments in Greek, including copies of Old Testament books and portions of the *Apocrypha and *Old Testament Pseudepigrapha, discovered in caves near the northwest edge of the Dead Sea in the 1940s. Many scholars believe the Essenes, a monastic, apocalyptically minded Jewish sect that lived at the site named Khirbet Qumran from the second century B.C. to the first century A.D. gathered and produced this literature.

deaspiration. *n.* The loss of *rough breathing when the following syllable contains an *aspirated consonant (φ, θ or ξ).

declension. *n.* A grouping of similarly inflected words (*see* inflection)—nouns, pronouns, adjectives or participles—according to a discernible pattern. Often grammars speak of three such patterns in Greek, termed *first, *second and *third declension.

declinable. *adj.* Capable of being *declined, included in a *declension or a grouping. This includes verbs, nouns and adjectives since they are *inflected according to their function. Some words do not undergo such inflectional changes and are therefore *indeclinable.

decline. *v.* Of certain words, to undergo alterations of *form (*see also* inflection); or to give the inflected forms of a word (*see* conjugate, parse).

deconstructionism. *n.* In biblical interpretation, analysis of the text that involves a "dismantling" of structures—linguistic, cultural, institutional, philosophical, political, etc. This entails recognizing, among other things, the incompleteness and inconsistencies of a text, the unfixed character of language, and perhaps even pessimism regarding the fruitfulness of interpretation.

deesis. *n.* An impassioned plea made in the name of an important figure, a god or a sacred object. See Romans 12:1.

defective verb. *n.* A verb that is not used in all three *voices; or a verb that uses a different *stem or stems to form its *tenses.

definite. *adj.* Of or pertaining to a specific, identifiable person, place, thing or entity, as in "*the* bear" (as opposed to "*a* bear," which is *indefinite).

definite article. *n.* A part of speech that particularizes (definitizes) a *substantive or a *clause. In English the definite article is *the*, as opposed to the indefinite article *a* or *an*. Greek has only the one article.

degrees. *n.* The classification of *adjectives according to whether they are *positive, *comparative or *superlative degree (e.g., *bright, brighter, brightest*).

deictic article. *n.* The use of the *article to specify a person or thing that is present at the time of speaking or writing. The article thus functions very much like the *near demonstrative in such cases (from δείκνυμι, "I point out").

deictic indicator. *See* deixis.

deixis. *n.* The ability of language, by means of a variety of features and indicators (deictic indicators—personal, temporal or locational), to place events in their relational contexts, including references to person, place and time. The name comes from the fact that deixis involves pointing to elements of the *cotext (the surrounding linguistic context) or the situational context beyond it.

deliberative. *adj.* Denoting calculation, intention or the consideration of options.

deliberative future. *n*. A future-tense verb that is used to ask a question. See Luke 22:49; John 6:68.

deliberative subjunctive. *n*. A subjunctive verb that is used in asking a question. See Luke 3:10; 11:5.

Delta Text. *See* Western text-type.

demonstrative. *See* demonstrative pronoun.

demonstrative adjective. *See* demonstrative pronoun.

demonstrative pronoun. *n*. A pronoun that serves as a pointer or indicates where something is in relation to the speaker/writer (Lat. *demonstrare*, "to point out"). *Near demonstratives (*this* and *these*) speak of things that are relatively close; *far demonstratives (*that* and *those*), of things that are relatively distant. The latter are sometimes distinguished as demonstrative adjectives.

demotic. *adj*. Pertaining to the common people; or more narrowly, pertaining to the *modern Greek *vernacular.

demythologization. *n*. The reinterpretation of biblical *myth (passages that speak of the transcendent, the world beyond, in this-worldly terms) so as to distill the essential truth from the imagery for modern people. Usually associated with the work of Rudolph Bultmann.

denial subjunctive. *See* emphatic negation subjunctive.

denominal. *See* denominative.

denominative. *adj*. Derived from a *noun. —*n*. A word (especially a verb) derived from a noun (e.g., τιμάω from τιμή). Also referred to as denominal.

denotation. *n*. The straightforward and explicit meaning of a word, the "dictionary definition." This term refers to the direct relationship between a word and that which it designates, which is in contrast to its *connotation, any secondary meaning that might be attached to it. Also known as unmarked, referential or cognitive meaning, as opposed to affective or connotative meaning.

denotative meaning. *See* denotation.

dental. *adj*. Articulated with the teeth. —*n*. A dental speech sound. Also called linguals.

dependent. *adj*. Used only in connection with other forms, never in isolation (except when the governing item is left unexpressed); subordinate.

dependent clause. *n*. A clause that cannot stand by itself but is *dependent on another. Also known as a subordinate clause.

deponent. *adj*. or *n*. A verb that has no *active form for a particular *principal part, but the force of which is active nevertheless (Lat. *deponere*, "to lay aside"). Deponent verbs are usually identifiable by their *lexical forms, which appear with passive endings (e.g., γίνομαι).

derivational morpheme. *n.* A *morpheme added to a word *stem, which changes its syntactic function (e.g., λαμπρός / λαμπρότης).

derivational morphology. *See* morphology.

derivative. *n.* A word that is derived from another word or words, especially from a different language. —*adj.* Denoting a derivative or the relationship of derivatives.

descriptive genitive. *n.* A genitive that provides a general description or characterization of its substantive. This is a very broad category since almost any genitive describes in some way; most genitives can be more narrowly defined. Also known as the adjective genitive.

descriptive grammar. *n.* Language study concerned simply with observing and describing linguistic phenomena, as opposed to *prescriptive grammar, which delineates rules for proper usage.

descriptive imperfect. *n.* A present-tense verb that is used of ongoing (progressive) action occurring in the past. Also known as the progressive imperfect.

descriptive present. *n.* A present-tense verb that is used of ongoing (progressive) action occurring in the present. Also known as the progressive present.

desiderative. *adj.* or *n.* Expressing a wish or a desire, often in the form of a command or plea (Lat. *desiderare*, "to desire").

Deuterocanonicals. *pl. n.* A term used by Catholics to designate books that were not in the Hebrew Bible but in the *Septuagint and that were later recognized as inspired. Others use the term *Apocrypha. The adjective *deuterocanonical* is also used broadly of passages that are considered to be later *accretions.

deutero-Pauline epistles. *pl. n.* The letters of Ephesians, Colossians, 2 Thessalonians and the Pastorals, which are considered by some to be "secondary" (hence "deutero"), reflecting *Pauline theology but written by an associate of Paul rather than the apostle. For some, the Pastorals are excluded from this definition. *See also Hauptbriefe* and undisputed Pauline epistles.

deverbative. *adj.* Derived from a *verb. —*n.* A word derived from a verb.

device. *n. See* literary device.

diachronic. *adj.* Pertaining to change over time (διά + χρόνος, "through time"). A diachronic word study investigates how the meaning of a term has evolved through different eras. A *synchronic study, on the other hand, observes different definitions or nuances of a word at a given time. Likewise, diachronic study of a text pertains to the stages by which the text came into being. *See also* synchronic, descriptive grammar, prescriptive grammar.

diacritic. *n. See* diacritical mark.

diacritic(al) mark. *n.* A symbol that attaches itself to a letter and either provides some additional information (as with the breathing marks) or alters its value (as with the accents). Sometimes called diacritical points.

diaeresis. *n.* In *orthography, the separation of two vowels that would normally form a *diphthong into two syllables, indicated by a *diacritical mark appearing as two dots over the second vowel; or the diacritical mark itself (e.g., ἰουδαϊσμός). In rhetoric, diaeresis occurs when roles are specified among several individuals in a group, or several parts of a whole (see 1 Cor 12:7-10). Also diaresis.

diagramming. *See* grammatical analysis.

dialect. *n.* A regional variety of a language that distinguishes itself to a significant degree but not enough to be considered a different language. Among the many dialects of ancient Greek, Attic was the most influential and is the ancestor of *Koine. It is often equated with "classical Greek" since it was the vehicle for many writers, including Aristophanes, Plato, Thucydides and Xenophon.

dialogue. *n.* A conversation. The term can also be used of rhetorical dialogue, in which a writer uses the first *person or converses with an imaginary partner. *See also* diatribe.

diaphora. *n.* Repetition of the same word, which takes on a slightly different significance each time. See Romans 3:21-26.

diaresis. *See* diaeresis.

Diatessaron. *n.* A *harmony of the life of Christ written by *Tatian in the second century, which survives only in fragments. It became the standard text of many Syriac-speaking churches until the fifth century.

diatribe. *n.* An ancient literary style that employs the device of an imaginary *dialogue partner or opponent, and which is often drawn out or acrimonious.

Didache n. A book of moral instruction (διδαχή), including a manual of church life and practice, written as if coming from the apostles (*The Teaching of the Lord Through the Twelve Apostles to the Nations*). *The Didache* is usually dated in the early second century. The term is sometimes used generally of catechetical material of the early church in contrast to *kerygma (preaching).

didactic. *adj.* Characterized by instruction, teaching or an abundance of *imperatives.

difficilior lectio potior. Lat. "The *more difficult reading is preferable."

difficult reading. *See* more difficult reading.

digamma. *n.* A Greek letter of the alphabet that dropped out by the time the New Testament was written. It looks like the capital letter "F" and was pronounced like "w." The presence of digamma can sometimes be felt in *irregular inflections.

diglossia. *n.* A situation in which high and low forms of a language are used; likewise a situation in which more than one language is used (e.g., in Palestine in the time of Jesus).

diglot. *n.* An edition of the Bible or a part of it that displays the text in two languages side by side for comparison. *See also* polyglot.

digraph. *n.* Two letters in sequence that represent a single speech sound (e.g., "sh" in *she*). Or conversely, a sound *cluster represented by a single letter (ζ, χ and ψ).

dikanische Gattungen. Germ. "decision texts."

diminutive. *adj.* Suggesting smallness, youth, affection or dismissal. —*n.* A diminutive *affix or name. In Greek, the suffixes -ιον and -ισκος form diminutive nouns (e.g., ἀρήν > ἀρνίον, "little lamb"; παῖς > παιδίον, "infant"). Also called hypocoristicon.

diphthong. *n.* Two vowels in sequence that are construed as a unit, a compound sound. Sometimes it is said that diphthongs have only one sound, but this is only the case with ου. It is more accurate to speak of two sounds (δι-, "two" + φθόγγος, "sound"), a vowel and a *glide. English has three clearly discernible diphthongs, exemplified in the words *rye, our* and *boy* (less conspicuous is the vowel sound in *may*). Greek contains these same diphthongs, written αι, αυ, οι and ει respectively, and others that are less common.

direct address. *n.* An address in which a noun or pronoun explicitly names the person or thing being addressed.

direct attraction. *See* attraction.

direct case. *See* oblique case.

direct discourse. *n.* The reporting of what someone has said by supplying the exact wording of the original statement. To mark direct discourse in English, quotation marks are used; in Greek one method is the *recitative ὅτι. The New Testament writers, by and large, prefer direct discourse to *indirect discourse. Also *oratio recta.* See Colossians 4:10.

direct equivalence. *n.* A theory of translation that operates under the assumption that there can—and should—be one-to-one correspondence between the particular words in the *source language and the *target language. *See also* dynamic equivalence, formal equivalence.

direct middle. *n.* The use of the middle voice to indicate that the subject acts upon itself.

direct object. *n.* The person or thing directly affected by the action of the verb.

direct question. *n.* A question reproduced in the precise form that it was asked in *direct discourse.

direct quotation. *n.* A quotation of the exact words of another. Also called a direct quote for short.

direct reflexive middle. *See* direct middle.

direct speech. *See* direct discourse.

discord. *n.* The lack of *agreement between the *forms of words where it would normally be expected. *See also* concord.

discourse. *n.* In linguistics, any segment of speech or writing longer than a sentence; or, likewise, a linguistic unit composed of several sentences.

discourse analysis. *n.* The study of larger units of speech and writing—anything above the sentence level—with special attentiveness to how writers employ certain linguistic features to achieve certain ends. The term can also be used with reference to recognizable "speech events" or types (e.g., a sermon, a joke, an interview), textual cohesion (how discourse units are bound together), argument development and the broad notion of text as social interchange. The term is sometimes used very broadly to entail study of practically all human communication. Also known as text grammar or text linguistics.

disjunctive. *adj.* Denoting contrast, opposition or pointing to an alternative. —*n.* A word that links contrastive clauses. The major disjunctive conjunction is ἤ, "or," but other words such as καί can occasionally carry the same force.

dislocated reading. *n.* In textual criticism, a *reading involving either *haplography or *dittography.

dissimilation. *n.* One consonant becoming less like an adjacent consonant. *See also* assimilation.

distinctive feature. *n.* In *phonology, a minimal property of a speech sound that provides the basis for contrast with other sounds (segmental contrasts).

distributive. *adj.* Referring to distribution or dispersal to individuals or component parts rather than to a group collectively. —*n.* A word that signifies distribution. See κατά in Luke 8:1, 4; Acts 15:21, 36; Titus 3:5; ἀνά with numbers in Luke 9:14; 10:1; Revelation 4:8.

dittography. *n.* The unintentional duplication of material in the copying of a *manuscript; the opposite of *haplography. Also dittograph.

divine passive. *n.* A verb in the passive voice with God as the implied *agent. Also referred to as the theological passive or *passivum divinum.* *See* Philemon 22.

documentary textual criticism. *See* genealogical method.

dominical saying. *n.* A saying of Jesus (Lat. *Dominus,* "Lord").

double accusative. *See* object complement construction.

double consonant. *n.* A consonant letter that represents two combined speech sounds (ζ, χ and ψ). *See also* digraph.

double negative. *n.* The occurrence of two or more negatives in a single construction, which may in English render the sentence ungrammatical but in Greek simply denotes strong negation. *See also* emphatic negation subjunctive.

double reading. *See* doublet.

double tradition. *n.* Common or similar material in two different sources; or more technically, material common to Matthew and Luke.

doublet. *n.* In Gospel criticism, a parallel saying or narrative that grew out of a single original statement or event. E.g., possibly the two versions of the feeding of the multitudes (one 5,000; the other, 4,000). Also referred to as a double reading.

dramatic aorist. *n.* An aorist tense used of an event that has just occurred or a state of mind just reached. See Matthew 9:18; Luke 16:4.

dramatic perfect. *See* aoristic perfect.

dramatic present. *See* historic(al) present.

dubitative subjunctive. *See* deliberative subjunctive.

durative. *adj.* Denoting action that is ongoing, progressive or continual.

dynamic equivalence. *n.* A theory of *translation that strives for the true sense of the *source language in translation but not necessarily for word-for-word correspondence. Such an approach recognizes that words are not to be confused with concepts (*see* word-concept fallacy) and treats reader impact with great significance so that what is aimed for is an "equivalence" of impression between the readers of the translation and the original readers. This notion is at the heart of communication theory. *See also* direct equivalence, formal equivalence.

dynamic middle. *See* indirect middle.

E

ecbatic. *adj.* Denoting result. The term is used in connection with a number of constructions, e.g., ἵνα clauses and verb tenses, as well as certain uses of the infinitive.

ecbatic aorist. *See* consummative aorist.

echo. *See* allusion.

eclectic method. *n.* An approach to textual criticism that seeks to identify the original biblical text not by looking to any one *manuscript or *text-type but by examining all the available variants and deciding among them. The result is an eclectic text. A rigorous eclectic method (*rigorous eclecticism) relies solely on *internal evidence; *reasoned eclecticism weighs *external evidence too.

eclectic text. *See* eclectic method.

eclecticism. *See* eclectic method.

edited text. *See* critical text.

editorial *we.* *n.* The use of the first-person *plural (we) for the first-person singular (I). Also called the epistolary plural and literary plural. See 2 Corinthians 10:11-15.

effective aorist. *See* consummative aorist.

Egyptian text-type. *See* Alexandrian text-type.

eight-case system. *n.* A way of understanding the Greek *case system that distinguishes eight cases (*nominative, *ablative, *genitive, *dative, *locative, *instrumental, *accusative and *vocative). The determination of the number of cases is based on their function; thus some of the cases are identical in form: ablative and genitive; likewise the dative, locative and instrumental. *See also* five-case system.

Einleitung. Germ. "introduction."

eisegesis. *n.* The mistake of reading meaning *into* a text rather than deriving meaning *from* it (used pejoratively, the opposite of *exegesis).

elative. *adj.* Of adjectives and adverbs, denoting intensity of *attribution. In Greek a *comparative or *superlative adjective or adverb, which would normally imply comparison, can actually make a *positive assertion. In such cases it is necessary to supply the word *very* to bring the sense across in English. Also called elative superlative.

elide. *v. See* elision.

elision. *n.* The omission of a portion of a word in pronunciation or writing. It normally refers to prepositions and particles losing a final short vowel when they appear immediately before a word that begins with a vowel. Elision is marked by an *apostrophe (e.g., δι᾽ αὐτοῦ). See Colossians 1:16; 4:15.

ellipse. *n.* An instance of *ellipsis, an omission.

ellipsis. *n.* The omission of an element of language that technically renders the sentence *ungrammatical but that is usually understood in context. Everyday speech is frequently elliptical. *See also* aposiopesis and brachylogy. See 1 Corinthians 10:24; 2 Corinthians 5:13; Ephesians 5:24; Philippians 2:5.

embedded. *adj.* Of words or sentences, included inside a construction.

emendation. *n.* A critical correction made to a manuscript. It can refer to an alteration based on a superior *reading in another text or to *conjectural emendation, a change made without direct textual support.

emphasis. *n.* Prominence given to an element of language. In Greek this can be achieved by a number of means, including deviating from normal word order; an emphatic word is often thrown forward in a sentence. See Ephesians 4:8.

emphatic negation subjunctive. *n.* An aorist subjunctive verb used with the *negatives οὐ and μή to express strong denial that something will occur. Also called the subjunctive in negative assertions.

enallage. *n.* The substitution of one grammatical *form (e.g., case, number, tense, etc.) for another (ἐν-αλλαγή, "interchange"). See Mark 5:15; 1 Thessalonians 3:11.

enargeia. *n.* In rhetoric, the narration of an incident as though it were present. See Galatians 2:1-11.

enclitic. *n.* A word that drops its accent and depends ("leans") on the preceding word for accent (ἐνκλιτικός, "leaning on"). Enclitic words include the indefinite pronoun, various particles and forms of εἰμί. *See also* proclitic.

encounter story. *n.* In the Gospels, a story in which a person is confronted by Jesus' claims.

ending. *n.* A meaningful grammatical element (*morpheme) affixed to the end of a word; or more narrowly, as shorthand for *case ending. Also known as termination or case termination. *See also* personal ending.

entailment. *n.* The relationship between two clauses or sentences, in which the truth of the one implies the truth of the other.

enumeratio. *See* merism.

epanadiplosis. *See* anaphora.

epanalepsis. *n.* The repetition of a word or group of words within the same clause. See Philippians 2:8.

epanaphora. *See* anaphora.

epanodos. *n.* The repetition of a sequence of words in reverse order or the return to the main point of a speech after a digression.

epanorthosis. *n.* In rhetoric, the rephrasing of an immediately preceding statement for qualification, correction or emphasis. See Romans 3:5.

epenthesis. *n.* The insertion of an extra sound or syllable within a word (ἔπεν, "up in" + τίθημι, "I place").

epexegetic(al). *adj.* Of conjunctions, genitives and infinitives, explanatory; drawing out the meaning of something. Also known as explanatory or explicative. See Colossians 1:5, 25; 2:8.

epexegetic(al) genitive. *See* genitive of apposition.

epexegeticus. Lat. "*epexegetic."

epideictic. *adj.* Demonstrating the oratorical skill of the speaker/writer.

epidiorthosis. *n.* A remark that concludes a difficult or unpalatable argument (see Rom 3:5; 1 Cor 7:6); or a correction or an apology added in retrospect. Such a statement, if it *precedes* the argument, is called *prodiorthosis.

epigram. *n.* A brief, pithy saying; or more narrowly, a short poem that expresses a moral truth.

epigraphy. *n.* The study of *inscriptions.

epimone. *n.* In rhetoric, repetition of the same thought two or more times using similar words or *synonyms (ἐπιμονή, "a dwelling upon"). See Mark 7:20-23; John 21:15-17; Romans 7:18-20; 1 Corinthians 13:4-8.

epiphonema. *n.* In rhetoric, a concluding statement that summarizes or finishes off an argument. See Galatians 3:1.

epiphora. *n.* *See* antistrophe.

episodic. *adj.* Comprised of loosely connected episodes. Or it can mean occasional or incidental.

epistle. *n.* A letter (ἐπιστολή). The term is applied to the majority of the New Testament writings, although there are obvious differences between a conventional letter and these writings.

epistolary aorist. *n.* An aorist tense verb that is past from the reader's point of view but actually present from the writer's point of view. Also called the *literary aorist. See Ephesians 6:22; 1 Corinthians 5:11; Philippians 2:28.

epistolary plural. *See* editorial *we.*

epistolography. *n.* The practice or study of letter composition.

epitheton. *n.* In rhetoric, a descriptive addition to a substantive, usually an adjective or a substantive in *apposition. See Philippians 2:25.

epitrochasmus. *n.* In rhetoric, a brief listing of topics, each of which could receive prolonged treatment, but which are merely cited. See

1 Corinthians 12:7-11; 2 Corinthians 11:23-27; Hebrews 11:32-38.

epitrope. *n.* In rhetoric, a challenge in which one's opponents are indulged or even dared to act contrary to the speaker/writer's position. See Galatians 3:2.

eponym. *n.* A personal noun from which a word has been derived. E.g., Constantine > Constantinople.

equative sentence. *n.* A sentence with an *equative verb as its *main verb.

equative verb. *n.* A verb that links two substantives and implies equality between them. The term is usually used with reference to εἰμί or γίνομαι when they function in this capacity. *See also* copula.

ergative active. *See* causative active.

erotesis. *n.* An affirmative proposition stated in the form of a *rhetorical question. See Mark 12:24; Romans 2:3-4.

errata. *pl. n.* A list of errors. Plural of erratum.

Essenes. *See* Dead Sea Scrolls.

ethical dative. *n.* A dative case substantive that designates the person for whom the verbal action is significant or whose point of view or opinion is tied to the action of the verb. This category can be subsumed under the *dative of reference. Also called the dative of feeling. E.g., ἀστεῖος τῷ θεῷ ("beautiful to God," Acts 7:20); also Philippians 1:21.

ethical list. *n.* A catalog of vices or virtues listed for exhortational purposes. *See also* vice list.

ethos. *n.* In rhetoric, with regard to theories of argument and persuasion, how a speaker establishes himself or herself as being trustworthy. *See also* logos and pathos.

etymological fallacy. *n.* The mistaken notion that the true meaning of a term lies in its primitive meaning (*etymology), that the earliest historical occurrence of a term yields the correct definition. It is a fallacy because the meanings of words evolve over time so that some words are quite detached from their origins. Also called root fallacy. *See also* illegitimate totality transfer.

etymology. *n.* The study of the derivation of words, both their forms and meanings. Also used of the product of such a study. *See also* etymological fallacy.

euphemism. *n.* The use of indirect or milder language when speaking about something that may cause offense.

euphony. *n.* A pleasing quality achieved in speech, that is, in the way it sounds.

Eusebian Canons. *n.* A set of tables (canons) compiled by Eusebius of

Caesarea (ca. 260-ca. 339), which provides the *parallel passages in the Gospels through a system of numbered paragraphs. *See also* kephalaia.

Evangelist. *n.* In Gospel studies, one of the writers of the Gospels.

ex itacismo. Lat. "by *itacism."

exaggeration. *n.* Distortion through overstatement for rhetorical effect. Exaggeration as a rhetorical device is not to be confused with embellishment or lying. *See* hyperbole.

exceptive. *adj.* Containing or denoting an exception or a condition.

excursus. *n.* A detailed discussion of a particular topic or point that is included in a book as a digression inserted in the text or appended at the end.

exegesis. *n.* The act or result of drawing out the meaning of the biblical text and explaining it; interpretation.

exegete. *n.* One who does *exegesis; an interpreter.

exemplar. *n.* A *manuscript that serves as the pattern from which a new copy is produced.

exhortatio. *n.* In rhetoric, an appeal designed to move the audience to accept one's thesis (*see* partitio) and the supporting arguments (*see* probatio) and take action. *See also* rhetorical criticism.

exhortation subjunctive. *See* hortatory subjunctive.

exhortative. *See* hortatory subjunctive.

exhortatory. *See* hortatory subjunctive.

exordium. *n.* In rhetoric, the introduction or *prologue. Exordium is one of several components of a classical oration. Also known as *prooemium. *See also* rhetorical criticism.

expanded text. *See* conflation.

expansion. *n.* In linguistics, an element added to a construction that does not modify the function of the preexisting elements or the basic structure.

explanatory. *adj.* Serving to explain. *See* epexegetical.

explanatory gloss. *See* gloss.

explicative. *See* epexegetical.

exposition. *n.* Biblical interpretation, with an emphasis on contemporary relevance and application.

extant. *adj.* Still in existence. The term is used positively of the large amount of New Testament *manuscript evidence and negatively of the *original documents, which are either lost or destroyed.

extensive perfect. *See* consummative perfect.

external evidence. *n.* The evidence pertaining to a particular *text-critical issue that arises from the *manuscripts and *versions themselves:

the quantity of the manuscript evidence on either side of an issue, the date and character of specific *witnesses, geographic distribution, etc. *See also* internal evidence.

extrabiblical. *adj.* Found outside the Bible.

extracanonical. *See* noncanonical.

F

factitive. *adj.* Of constructions and words (especially verbs), denoting action in which a cause produces a result. Thus a factitive verb takes a *direct object and an *object complement, with the construction carrying a causative/resultative idea (e.g., *made* in "Jeff made him angry."). See Luke 19:46.

factive. *adj.* Of words and phrases, asserting a fact. The opposite of factive is nonfactive.

family. *n.* In textual criticism, a group of *manuscripts similar enough in their variations that they are considered to have the same origin. The term is used more narrowly than *text-type to describe manuscripts that are very similar to one another.

far demonstrative. *n.* A *demonstrative pronoun that functions to specify that the substantive it refers to is relatively distant from the speaker/writer, e.g., *that* and *those*. *See also* near demonstrative.

Farrer hypothesis. *n.* A proposed solution to the *synoptic problem that suggests that Mark was written first; then Matthew second, without depending on sources; and Luke, depending on Matthew, was third.

feminine. *adj.* Designating one of three *genders in Greek (the others being masculine and neuter). —*n.* A feminine word. Since Greek for the most part follows *grammatical gender rather than *natural gender, there is rarely any discernible explanation for why a word is a particular gender.

feminist criticism. *n.* Interpretation of texts that is expressly from the standpoint of women and that, through a variety of critical methods, focuses on issues such as culturally based presuppositions, the way texts are "gendered," the participation of women in society, political and theological alliances, social identities and locations, institutional structures, and other matters related to ideologies of gender, sexuality and power. Similarly, womanist interpretation has been taken up by many women of color, especially black women, with special emphasis on issues of racism, sexism and class structures.

Festschrift. *n.* A publication celebrating an event or honoring a senior scholar. *Festschriften* are often compilations of essays by several authors published on the occasion of a colleague's birthday or retirement.

figura etymologica. *See* cognate accusative.

figurative. *adj.* Involving a *nonliteral, metaphorical or symbolic sense, or containing *figures of speech. The term is used in a number of ways to refer to speech or writing that for some reason cannot be interpreted in a strictly *literal sense.

figure of speech. *n.* A rhetorical device that uses language in a distinctive, often *nonliteral way to achieve a particular effect. The term is sometimes reserved for formal rhetorical devices such as metaphor and *hendiadys, etc., or it can include other less formal uses of language.

filler. *n.* In linguistics, a word or form that can be used in a particular place (i.e., a *slot) in a grammatical construction.

final. *adj.* Denoting purpose. The term is used of infinitives, participles, particles, subjunctives and whole clauses. Also referred to as telic or purpose.

final clause. *n.* A clause that denotes purpose, as in "Lisa waited by the exit *in order to get her autograph.*"

finite verb. *n.* A verb that limits the action to a specific *subject (i.e., it has *person), such as those in the indicative, subjunctive, imperative and optative moods. This is in contrast to infinitives and participles, which technically do not limit the action to a specific subject.

first aorist. *n.* A verb that in the aorist tense behaves according to an observable pattern in its *inflections; it normally uses a *tense stem that is identical to the *present-tense stem, and it uses an "infixed" sigma as a *tense formative. Whether a verb is a first aorist or a *second aorist has no bearing on its meaning; rather, aorist verbs happen to decline according to two clearly identifiable patterns, and they are compartmentalized this way to aid the student.

first attributive position. *n.* The position of an adjective when it appears in the sequence article-adjective-noun.

first class condition. *n.* A *conditional sentence in which the premise of the *protasis (the "if" clause) is assumed to be true or is presented as true for the sake of argument. This is conveyed by using εἰ plus a verb in the indicative mood in the protasis and any mood or tense in the *apodosis (the "then" clause). Also called the simple condition.

first declension. *n.* The inflectional pattern (*see* inflection) for words whose *stems end in α or η (comprised mostly of feminine words).

first predicate position. *n.* The position of an adjective when it appears in the sequence adjective-article-noun.

five-case system. *n.* A way of understanding the Greek language, based on formal rather than functional considerations, that distinguishes five *cases: *nominative, *genitive, *dative, *accusative and *vocative. *See also* eight-case system.

florilegium. *n.* A collection of excerpts from prior writings; an anthology (Lat. "gathering of flowers"). Some of the documents from the *Dead Sea Scrolls are florilegia (e.g., 4QFlor, 4QTest). Scriptural florilegia are called catenae.

folio. *n.* A piece of paper folded once in the middle, making four pages; a book consisting of such sheets (Lat. *folium*, "leaf").

foregrounding. *v.* or *n.* The giving of prominence to a linguistic element. *See also* backgrounding.

form. *n.* As a grammatical term, an inflected word (*see* inflect, inflection); or a word as it appears in a given context with reference to its inflectional characteristics. With regard to texts, the *genre, organization, rhetorical and *literary devices, etc. used in presenting the material, in contrast to the content or meaning conveyed by the text's form. *See also* formalism, New Criticism.

form criticism. *n.* The discipline concerned with the stories about Jesus and his teaching in their pre-literary state; how these distinct units of material arose out of certain cultural contexts according to identifiable *forms and were transmitted by the early church. Translation of the German *Formgeschichte*.

form word. *See* function word.

formal equivalence. *n.* An approach to *translation that seeks to reproduce the original with great literalness, including sentence structure and word order; or the end product in such a translation. *See also* direct equivalence, dynamic equivalence.

formal preposition. *n.* A preposition that can only function as a preposition, as opposed to a functional preposition, which can be used in another capacity.

formalism. *n.* An approach to textual interpretation that emphasizes analysis of formal features, *literary techniques and internal structures of the text. In formalism, what counts is in the text, as opposed to reader-oriented approaches. Formalism is usually associated with *structuralism, literary-rhetorical criticism and New Criticism.

formative lengthening. *See* lengthening.

Formgeschichte. Germ. "form history." *See* form criticism.

formula. *n.* A short, fixed, *literary form established through repeated use to introduce or signal a larger form. E.g., prophetic formula ("Thus says the Lord"); formula of asseveration ("Truly I say to you"). Also formulary.

Four-Source hypothesis. *n.* A proposed solution to the *synoptic problem that asserts that Mark and three hypothetical sources—*Q, *L and *M—lie behind Matthew and Luke. Also known as the Four-Document hypothesis or the *Oxford hypothesis.

fourth class condition. *n.* A *conditional sentence in which the premise of the *protasis (the "if" clause) is presented as possible but unlikely. This is conveyed by using εἰ plus an optative mood verb in the protasis and ἄν plus the optative in the *apodosis (the "then" clause). Also called less probable future condition.

free form. *See* free morpheme.

free morpheme. *n.* A meaningful speech unit (*morpheme) that can be used as a word without modification or attachment to another form, as opposed to a *bound morpheme.

frequentative. *See* iterative.

fricative. *n.* A speech sound articulated by narrowing the vocal apparatus to partially obstruct the airstream and produce audible friction. In Greek, θ, φ, σ, ξ and the rough breathing. Also called spirants.

front. *adj.* Of speech sounds, articulated at the front of the mouth. Front vowels, for example, involve the front part of the tongue.

front-clipping. *See* aphesis.

function word. *n.* A word that primarily serves as a grammatical *structure marker (e.g., articles, conjunctions) in contrast to one that carries strong *lexical meaning. Also called form words or markers.

functional preposition. *n.* A word that can function as a *preposition and in another capacity.

fusional language. *See* inflected language.

future. *n.* The *tense that normally expresses verbal action occurring in the future in relation to the speaker/writer. This tense is also used in contexts in which the verbal action is *voluntative, *gnomic or *deliberative.

future perfect tense. *n.* A *periphrastic construction that contains a future form of εἰμί plus a perfect participle, which denotes completed action in the future. See Matthew 16:19; 18:18; Hebrews 2:13.

futuristic aorist. *See* proleptic aorist.

futuristic present. *n.* A present-tense verb that describes future action. See Matthew 17:11; John 4:25.

G

gamma nasal. *n.* A gamma (γ) that is immediately followed by another gamma (or any letter pronounced in the same place in the mouth, the *velum), which changes the pronunciation of the first gamma from a "hard g" sound (as in *gap*) to an "n" or "ng" sound.

Gattung. Germ. "form; type; *genre." *pl. Gattungen.*

Gattungforschung. Germ. "genre research." *See* genre, genre criticism.

Gemara. *n.* *Commentary on the *Mishnah written by rabbis called the Amoraim (expounders), including exposition, descriptions of customs, proverbs, rabbinic folklore, etc. (Heb. "teaching, instruction"). Gemara primarily came from two centers, Babylon and Palestine, from the third to the fifth centuries.

gematria. *n.* A Jewish method of interpreting the deeper meaning of words based on the numerical value of their individual letters. In both Hebrew and Greek, letters also serve as numbers.

Gemeinde. Germ. "congregation, community" (often the *believing* community).

geminate. *n.* A sequence of identical adjacent speech sounds in a single *morpheme.

gemination. *n.* The doubling of a consonant.

gender. *n.* The component of language that attaches to words the distinction of either *male, *female or *neuter, though these classifications may or may not correspond to *actual* gender. In Greek, adjectives and participles change gender according to usage, but *nouns retain their gender in all circumstances. *See* grammatical gender and natural gender.

genealogical method. *n.* An approach to *textual criticism that involves attempting to reconstruct the history of the New Testament text by organizing all *extant *manuscripts into groups or clusters, tracing lines of *transmission and identifying chronological succession, isolating the earliest stages and then choosing the earliest *readings. Also called documentary textual criticism, the historical-documentary method or the historical-genealogical method. The term can also refer to the reconstruction of a particular *stemma for a variant. Also referred to as the stemmatic method.

genealogical principle. *n.* In textual criticism, the guiding rule that *manuscripts must be weighed rather than counted.

genealogical solidarity. *n.* Uniformity among the *witnesses for a particular variant with regard to their *text-types and text *families.

General Epistles. *n. See* Catholic Epistles.

general present. *See* customary present.

generalizing plural. *n.* A plural that actually refers to a singular subject. See Matthew 2:20, 23. The opposite of the generalizing plural is the *generic singular.

generative grammar. *n.* A set of *grammatical rules that specifies, defines and reduces the potentially infinite number of sentences in a language to a finite set.

generic. *adj.* Of a particular group, class or category (Lat. *genus*). See Colossians 3:18.

generic singular. *n.* A singular noun that actually refers to a group or class, or a multiplicity of things. See Colossians 1:10.

generic term. *n.* A word that, despite being gender-specific (ordinarily denoting the male gender), actually specifies neither masculine, neuter or feminine gender. E.g., *mankind.*

genetically related. *adj.* Of languages, developing from a common, earlier language. In textual criticism it refers to texts or textual features that signify a common ancestry.

genitival. *adj.* Of or pertaining to a genitive.

genitive. *adj.* or *n.* The *case that normally limits the quality of *substantives as to their kind, class or category, often denoting possession, source or concepts conveyed in English by the preposition *of.* The genitive often answers the question, "What kind?"

genitive absolute. *n.* A clause that contains a participle and (almost always) a substantive, both in the genitive case, and that is usually grammatically unrelated to the rest of the sentence (i.e., *absolute). See Matthew 8:1; Romans 7:3.

genitive chain. *n.* A string of genitives. Normally in such cases each genitive depends on the preceding one. Also called concatenative genitives.

genitive of agency. *n.* A genitive substantive denoting a personal *agent. E.g., διδακτοὶ θεοῦ ("taught by God," Jn 6:45); also 1 Corinthians 2:13.

genitive of apposition. *n.* A genitive that refers back to its own substantive—to the same person or thing (or a category to which it belongs), as in "city of Jerusalem" or "sign of circumcision." Also called the genitive of definition or identity, or the appositional genitive (see Rom 4:11; 2 Pet 2:6). Sometimes genitives in *simple* apposition—when the substantive and genitive refer to *exactly* the same thing—are distinguished (see Mt 2:11; Tit 2:13).

genitive of comparison. *n.* A genitive noun that invites comparison by supplying something as a standard of comparison. See John 14:28; Hebrews 1:4; 7:26. Also called comparative genitive.

genitive of content. *n.* A genitive substantive that specifies the contents of the word that governs it. See Luke 4:28; John 21:8; Acts 6:3; Colossians 2:3.

genitive of definition. *See* genitive of apposition.

genitive of description. *See* descriptive genitive.

genitive of destination. *n.* A genitive substantive that indicates the direction the *head noun is moving or its destination or purpose. Also known as genitive of direction. E.g., ὁδὸν σωτηρίας ("way of salvation," Acts 16:17).

genitive of direction. *See* genitive of destination.

genitive of material. *n.* A genitive substantive that specifies the material of which the *head noun consists. E.g., ἐπίβλημα ῥάκους ἀγνάφου ("a patch of unshrunk cloth," Mk 2:21). In some grammars this category is subsumed under the *genitive of apposition. Also called *genitivus materiae*.

genitive of means. *n.* A genitive substantive that denotes means in regard to the verbal action implied in the *head noun (or the verb itself). E.g., οὐκ ἐν διδακτοῖς ἀνθρωπίνης σοφίας λόγοις ("not in words taught by human wisdom," 1 Cor 2:13); also Philippians 2:8.

genitive of origin/source. *n.* A genitive substantive denoting the origin from which the *head noun derives. E.g., ἐπιστολὴ Χριστοῦ ("a letter from Christ," 2 Cor 3:3); also Philippians 4:7.

genitive of place. *n.* A genitive substantive indicating the location of the verbal action (the action of the *verb to which the genitive is related). E.g., ὕδατος ("in water," Lk 16:24); also 1 Corinthians 4:5.

genitive of price/value. *n.* A genitive substantive that designates the price paid or the value assessed for the *head noun (or other word) to which it is related. See Matthew 20:13; 2 Thessalonians 1:5, 11; 1 Timothy 5:17.

genitive of product. *n.* A genitive substantive that denotes that which is produced by the *head noun. This category can be subsumed by the *objective genitive. See Romans 15:13, 33.

genitive of production. *n.* A genitive substantive that indicates that which is the maker or producer of the *head noun. See Ephesians 4:3; Philippians 2:8.

genitive of purpose. *n.* A genitive substantive that denotes the purpose of the *head noun's existence. Sometimes subsumed under the *genitive of destination. E.g., ἀνάστασιν ζωῆς ("resurrection that leads to life," Jn 5:29).

genitive of quality. *See* attributive genitive.

genitive of reference. *n.* A genitive substantive that denotes the idea of reference. See Hebrews 3:12; 5:13

genitive of relationship. *n.* A genitive substantive that indicates a familial relationship. Sometimes treated along with the *genitive of origin/ source. See Luke 24:10; John 21:15.

genitive of separation. *n.* A genitive substantive denoting separation; the genitive provides the point of departure. E.g., ἐκτινάξατε τὸν κονιορτὸν τῶν ποδῶν ὑμῶν ("shake off the dust from your feet," Mt 10:14).

genitive of source. *See* genitive of origin/source.

genitive of subordination. *n.* A genitive substantive that indicates that which is subordinated to the *head noun. Sometimes subsumed under the *objective genitive. See Matthew 9:34; 2 Corinthians 4:4.

genitive of the divided whole. *See* partitive genitive.

genitive of time. *n.* A genitive substantive that delineates an amount of time. See Luke 18:12; John 3:2; 1 Thessalonians 2:9.

genitivus materiae. See genitive of material.

genre. *n.* a standardized category of *literary composition involving form, *style and subject matter, which sustains and dictates an entire literary work. *See also* subgenre.

genre criticism. *n.* The discipline concerned with identifying and analyzing *genre, which normally involves paying attention to the form, *style and content of a *literary work, as well as its function.

genuine eclecticism. *See* reasoned eclecticism.

geographical distribution. *n.* In textual criticism, the combination of *witnesses from multiple *text-types for a particular variant.

gerund. *n.* In English grammar, a verbal *form ending in *-ing* that functions as a *noun. Greek has no gerund forms, but the *infinitive, as a verbal noun, is largely equivalent.

Geschichte. Germ. "history." —*n.* The term pertains to the significance of events for faith, as opposed to *Historie, what transpires objectively.

gezerah shawa. n. One of the rules or techniques of midrashic interpretation (*see* midrash), which says that where the same words are present in two texts, the same considerations apply (Heb. "an equivalent regulation"). The term is often used of biblical *citations in which a writer has appealed to verbal similarity. Also *gezera;* also *sawa* and *sawah.*

glide. *n.* A transitional speech sound articulated as the vocal organs move toward or away from the articulation of another speech sound.

global aorist. *See* constative aorist.

gloss. *n.* or *v.* A brief explanation or additional note. The term can refer to an explanatory comment written in the margin of a *manuscript or between the lines (an interlinear gloss). Occasionally these were even incorporated into the text itself (see Jn 5:3b-4; Rom 8:1). Bibles with patristic glosses became popular and somewhat standardized in the Middle Ages, particularly the *Glossa Ordinaria*. Similarly, it refers to a short definition that is helpful for learning a new or difficult word, but which may not reflect the wider range of meaning of the word. Sometimes *gloss* is a technical term for a statement or passage that was evidently added secondarily to a text.

Glossa Ordinaria. *n.* A *commentary on Scripture that consisted of *glosses (marginal comments) culled from patristic writers and popularized in the Middle Ages (Lat. "ordinary gloss"). Sometimes simply referred to as *The Gloss*.

glossator. *n.* A person who writes *glosses. Also glossarist.

glottal stop. *n.* A speech sound involving full closure of the glottis with audible release; or the closure itself.

gnome. *n.* A truism or maxim that is often well known by one's audience, used for support of an argument (γνώμη, "maxim"). See 2 Corinthians 9:7.

gnomic. *adj.* Marked by short expressions of wisdom, truth or principle; aphoristic (γνώμη, "maxim"). The term is used of certain verb tense uses—the aorist, future and present specifically—when a general, timeless truth is given, as in "The wind blows where it wants to" (Jn 3:8). Also referred to as omnitemporal.

goal. *n.* In linguistics, that which is affected by the action of the verb or that to/at which the action of the verb is directed.

gospel, Gospel. *n.* The good news of Jesus Christ; a book relating the Christian message; one of the four canonical Gospels; a literary *genre.

gospel criticism. *n.* The application of critical methods to the Gospels.

Gospel of Thomas. *n.* A second-century "sayings gospel" (a collection of short sayings without narrative), of which a complete Coptic copy was discovered at *Nag Hammadi in Egypt in 1945.

governing noun. *See* head noun.

gradation. *See* vowel gradation.

grammar. *n.* The study of the components of language; or a book that discusses grammar.

grammatical. *adj.* Conforming to the rules of *syntax; or more generally, related to *grammar.

grammatical analysis. *n.* Dissection of a unit of writing involving the parsing of *forms, classification of terms according to their function, and often a mechanical layout or diagram that depicts syntactical relationships.

grammatical gender. *n.* The designation of the *gender of words—whether masculine, feminine or neuter—not based on whether the objects in question are truly male or female (called *natural gender) but solely based on *grammatical usage.

grammaticalize. *v.* To signify a particular semantic sense morphologically (i.e., by *form).

grammatico-historical exegesis. *n.* Biblical interpretation that seeks to understand the text on a grammatical/syntactical level, as well as situated in its historical context. This approach often seeks primarily to know what the author intended in the text and what it meant to its first recipients. Sometimes called grammatico-historical criticism.

Granville Sharp construction. *n.* The construction article-substantive-καί-substantive (signified by TSKS). *See* Granville Sharp rule.

Granville Sharp rule. *n.* A grammatical dictum stating that when two or more personal, singular substantives (not proper names) are joined by καί and governed by a single article, they refer to the same person. This type of construction is often signified by TSKS.

grapheme. *n.* The symbols (letters) of an alphabetic writing system.

grave accent. *n.* An accent that appears as a backward-slanted mark above vowels (τὴν) and was originally used to signify a drop in pitch (Lat. *gravis*, "heavy").

Greek. *n.* An *Indo-European language that has existed in some form for thousands of years. *See also* biblical Greek, classical Greek, Hellenistic Greek, Indo-European and Koine.

Griesbach hypothesis. *n.* A proposed solution to the *synoptic problem that asserts that Matthew was written first; then Luke, depending on Matthew; then Mark, depending on both. Articulated by J. J. Griesbach (1745-1812). Also referred to as the Two-Gospel hypothesis. *See also* Augustinian hypothesis.

H

habitual present. *See* customary present.

haggadah. *n.* Jewish teaching on nonlegal matters. Sometimes aggadah. The counterpart of *halakhah.

haggadic midrash. *See* midrash.

halakhah. *n.* Jewish teaching on matters of conduct that are preserved in the *Talmud, the *Mishnah and various midrashim (*see* midrash). The counterpart of *haggadah.

halakic midrash. *See* midrash. (Also spelled halakhic.)

hand. *n.* A *scribe or *copyist, someone who has "a hand" in the production of a *manuscript. A reference to the first and second hand, and so on, denotes the scribe who first produced a manuscript (also known as the original hand) and then a *corrector, respectively.

hanging nominative. *See* pendent nominative.

hapax legomenon. *n.* A word that appears only once in a designated document or body of literature (ἄπαξ λεγόμενον, "something said once"). *pl.* hapax legomena.

haplography. *n.* The unintentional omission of material in the copying of a *manuscript. Sometimes as a result of *parablepsis. It is the opposite of *dittography. Matthew 12:47; Luke 10:32; 14:27; John 17:15; 1 Corinthians 9:2.

harder reading. *See* more difficult reading.

hardship list. *n.* A catalogue of misfortunes or trials, as found in Greek philosophical literature, Jewish writings and the New Testament. Also called affliction list and peristasis catalog. See Romans 8:35-39; 1 Corinthians 4:9-13; 2 Corinthians 4:8-9; 6:4-10; 11:23-28; Philippians 4:11-12; 2 Timothy 3:11.

harmonization. *n.* In the process of copying, the alteration of the biblical text to smooth over difficulties or apparent discrepancies. E.g., Matthew 15:8; 19:17; Luke 11:2-4; John 19:20; Acts 9:5-6; Romans 13:9; Colossians 1:14; Revelation 1:5. The term is also used in biblical interpretation when discrepant texts are in some way reconciled.

harmony of the Gospels. *n.* A book that blends the four *Gospels into a single story. The first harmony was *Tatian's *Diatessaron. Sometimes the word is used synonymously with *synopsis.

Hauptbriefe. Germ. "main letters." —*pl. n.* Usually refers to Paul's four capital *epistles: Galatians, Romans, and 1 and 2 Corinthians. *See also* deutero-Pauline epistles and undisputed Pauline epistles.

Haustafeln. Germ. "household codes" (lit. "house tables"). *sg. Haustafel.* *See* household code(s).

head. *n.* The central or governing element in a phrase, which determines any relationship of *concord, and which, when stripped of its *modifiers, has the same grammatical function as the construction as a whole (i.e., it is distributionally equivalent to the phrase). Also called the head term.

head noun. *n.* The substantive on which other elements in a construction are *dependent (*see* head); or more narrowly, the governing noun in a *genitival construction. Also called the *nomen regens*.

Hebraism. *n.* A characteristic of Hebrew idiom that resonates in the Greek of the *Septuagint or the New Testament. *See also* Aramaism, Semitism.

Hebrew genitive. *See* attributive genitive.

Heilsgeschichte. Germ. "*salvation-history."

Hellenistic Greek. *n.* The Greek language as it existed from the time of Alexander the Great (3rd cent. B.C.) to the time of the writing of the New Testament and beyond. It was given this name because its expansion ran parallel to Hellenization, the spread of Greek culture. It is used synonymously with *Koine Greek.

Hellenistic period. *n.* The era during which *Hellenistic Greek thrived, roughly 300 B.C. to A.D. 300. Also called the Koine period. *See* Hellenistic Greek.

helping verb. *See* auxiliary verb.

helps for readers. *n.* The different types of aids that have been introduced at various times in the history of New Testament *manuscript production, including chapter divisions, chapter titles and punctuation.

hendiadys. *n.* The use of two words to express a single concept (ἐν διὰ δυοῖν, "one by means of two"), as in "I was battered and beaten." Often one of the terms is actually *dependent on the other and can be turned into an adjective, as in "one is struck by his passion and his singing" with the sense of "passionate singing." See Colossians 1:9; 2:5; 2 Peter 1:3.

hermeneutical circle. *n.* The truism that very often the parts of a text can only be understood in light of the whole, and yet the whole can only be understood in light of the parts.

hermeneutics. *n.* The discipline of interpreting texts, with special reference to the principles and procedures involved (ἑρμηνεύω, "translate, interpret").

Hesychian text-type. *See* Alexandrian text-type.

heteroclisis. *n.* Fluctuation in the *declensions or inflectional patterns of certain *irregular words. Sometimes used synonymously with *metaplasm.

heteronym. *n.* One of two or more words that are spelled the same but have different meanings (and are sometimes pronounced differently), as in *row,* "a line," and *row,* "to propel a boat." Synonymous with *homograph.

heterophone. *n.* One of two or more words that are spelled the same but are pronounced differently and have different meanings, as in the noun *minute,* a unit of time, and the adjective *minute,* meaning very small. Heterophones are a subset of *heteronyms.

heterorganic. *adj.* Of speech sounds, produced at different places of articulation. The opposite of *homorganic.

Hexapla. *n.* The title of Origen's critical edition of the Old Testament, which contained six parallel columns: Hebrew; a Greek *transliteration; *Aquila; Symmachus; the *Septuagint; and *Theodotion. It survives only in fragments.

Hexaplaric. *adj.* Of textual corruptions derived from the *Hexapla.

hiatus. *n.* The coming together of two vowels in successive words, without *contraction, as in "Be eager." A number of classical writers tended to avoid hiatus; some detect this same tendency in the book of Hebrews.

higher criticism. *n.* A term that refers to all forms of *biblical criticism (*form criticism, *redaction criticism, etc.) with the exception of *textual criticism (termed *lower criticism). The term is no longer widely used.

historic(al) perfect. *See* aoristic perfect.

historic(al) present. *n.* The use of a present tense verb to describe past action. Certain New Testament writers are more fond of using the historic present than others. See Mark 11:27; John 18:28.

historical aorist. *See* constative aorist.

historical criticism. *n.* The discipline concerned with the historical situation that gave rise to the biblical writings as well as the historicity of events described in the text.

historical linguistics. *See* philology.

historical-critical method. *See* historical criticism.

historical-documentary method. *See* genealogical method.

historical-genealogical method. *See* genealogical method.

Historie. Germ. "history." —*n.* The term refers to objective, verifiable historical occurrences, in contrast to *Geschichte. See also Heilsgeschichte.*

historiography. *n.* The writing of history; historical literature; or the methodology of historical study.

Hochliteratur. Germ. "high literature." —*n.* Formal *literary works, as opposed to popular storytelling. *See also Kleinliteratur.*

holistic reading. *n.* Interpretation of biblical texts that takes them as they stand (as finished wholes), rather than reducing them to preexisting parts, which are then interpreted individually or in a manner that detracts from the unity of the whole composition.

homograph. *n.* One of two or more words that are identical in spelling but different in meaning and pronunciation (e.g., *lead* = "guide" vs. *lead* = the metal). Homographs are a subset of a *homonyms.

homoioarchton. *n.* An unintentional error of eyesight committed when copying the biblical text, due to words or lines that begin similarly. Also homoioarcton. *See also* parablepsis.

homoiomeson. *n.* An unintentional error of eyesight committed when copying the biblical text, due to words or lines that are similar in the middle. *See also* parablepsis.

homoioptoton. *n.* Repetition of the same grammatical *case within a single sentence/*period; or ending several clauses with words in the same case. See Romans 12:11-12.

homoioteleuton. *n.* In textual criticism, an unintentional error of eyesight committed when copying the biblical text, due to words or lines that end similarly. In rhetoric, homoioteleuton involves *coordinate clauses that end in similar words (see Rom 12:15). Also homoeoteleuton. *See also* parablepsis.

homologoumena. *n.* The group of writings that were undisputed during the first three centuries of church history and ultimately accepted into the New Testament *canon (in contrast with the antilegomena). Also homologumena. *See also* antilegomenon.

homonym. *n.* One of two or more words that sound the same when pronounced (and are often spelled the same) but have different meanings. Dictionaries differentiate between homonymy, in which words do not have a shared *etymology, and *polysemy, in which they do. Polysemous words are usually treated in one entry (but numbered separately), and homonymous words have separate entries.

homophone. *n.* One of two or more words that sound the same when pronounced but are spelled differently and are different in meaning, as in *wine* (as in Chardonnay) and *whine* (to complain). Homophones are a subset of *homonyms.

homorganic. *adj.* Of speech sounds, produced at the same place of articulation. The opposite of *heterorganic.

hortative. *See* hortatory subjunctive.

hortatory subjunctive. *n.* A first-person plural subjunctive that serves as an exhortation to oneself and others (usually translated "let us"). There are a handful of hortatory subjunctives that are singular ("let me"). Also referred to as the cohortative, hortative, volitive, exhortative, exhortation and exhortatory subjunctive. See Hebrews 12:1; 1 John 4:7.

household code(s). *n.* Rules governing domestic relationships: husbands and wives; parents and children; masters and slaves. See Romans 13:1-4; Ephesians 5:18—6:9; Colossians 3:18—4:6; 1 Peter 2:13—3:7. Also called household duty codes, household rules or *Haustafeln.*

hymnic. *adj.* Pertaining to or derived from a hymn. *See also carmina.*

hypallage. *n.* The reversal of the expected syntactic relation between two words for rhetorical effect.

hyperbaton. *n.* The separation of words that naturally belong together, for *emphasis; or the movement of a word or clause from its normal and expected place (ὑπερβατόν, "transposed"). E.g., in Matthew 3:10 ἤδη is separated from its verb.

hyperbole. *n.* The intentional use of *exaggeration or overstatement for *emphasis (ὑπερβολή, "extravagance"). Hyperbole can also take conventional forms, understood by native speakers, which do not necessarily connote emphasis. See Matthew 6:24; 10:37; Luke 14:26; John 21:25; Galatians 1:8; Colossians 1:23; Philemon 16.

hypocorism. *n.* A name of endearment. *See also* diminutive.

hypocoristicon. *See* diminutive.

hyponema. *n.* In ancient texts, a series of notes on the meaning of the text (Gk. "commentary"). *pl.* hyponemata.

hypotactic. *adj.* Of words and clauses, subordinate; or of writing style more generally, containing a fair amount of subordinated elements. *See* hypotaxis.

hypotaxis. *n.* The subordinate relationship of clauses (ὑποτάσσω, "place under"). The opposite of *parataxis.

hysterologia. *n.* In rhetoric, a statement that places the logically prior subject last and the logically ultimate subject first. See Ephesians 6:12.

hysteron proteron. Lat. "latter first." —*n.* An inversion of words or *phrases that reverses the natural order of temporal elements (see Jn 1:51). In logic, it refers to a premise that was not actually proved.

I

identical adjective. *n.* The *adjectival use of αὐτός to mean "same." For example, when Jesus repeated himself in prayer in Mark 14:39 he said τὸν αὐτὸν λόγον, "the same word."

ideological criticism. *n.* Criticism of texts that pays special attention to the way meaning is created in and by social, cultural and political realities, and to the role and character of language in conveying meaning, often with emphasis on issues related to power and liberation, particularly Marxist themes.

idiolect. *n.* The language usage of an individual, considered by linguists to be at least on some level unique to that person.

idiom. *n.* A fairly fixed speech form or expression that cannot be understood grammatically from its constituents parts but whose elements function as a set with a meaning peculiar to itself (ἴδιος, "one's own").

idiomatic participle. *See* redundant participle.

illative. *adj.* Pertaining to an inference. —*n.* An *inferential word or phrase. Also inferential.

illegitimate totality transfer. *n.* The error of taking the conclusions of a word study—observing the various meanings of a word over time and in different contexts—and assuming them all to be present in a single contextual usage of that word. *See also* etymological fallacy.

ill-formed. *See* ungrammatical.

illocutionary act. *n.* In linguistics, a speech form that performs an action by virtue of its being spoken (e.g., promising, commanding, requesting) or that calls for action. *See also* speech-act theory and performative language.

imperatival future. *n.* A future tense indicative verb that expresses a command, as in "You will not go outside of the house today." See James 2:8.

imperative. *n.* The *mood that normally expresses a command or some similar declaration of volition. Mood expresses the character of a verb as far as its actuality or potentiality; in the imperative mood, the one giving the command speaks to something that is in the realm of the possible and makes it known that he or she wants this to be actualized.

imperfect. *adj.* or *n.* The verb *tense that normally denotes progressive (ongoing) past action.

imperfective. *adj.* Pertaining to verbal action that is in progress.

impersonal verb. *n.* The use of a verb for which no real *subject can be found except *it* as in "it is quite late." E.g., δεῖ, "it is necessary"; ἀνήκει, "it is appropriate."

implicature. *n.* In linguistics, analysis of the implications or secondary meanings of expression, which may not be on the surface of a text or utterance (the primary meaning) but which are nevertheless understood.

imprecation optative. *See* curse optative.

improper diphthong. *n.* A vowel with an *iota subscript underneath it, which is pronounced as if the iota were not there.

improper preposition. *n.* An adverb or noun in a particular case (normally genitive) that functions like a *preposition. They are improper only in the sense that they differ from the other prepositions and because their frequent usage is a peculiarity of the *Hellenistic period. The most common improper prepositions include ἕως, ἐνώπιον, ἄχρι and ἔμπροσθεν (all with the genitive). Sometimes called adverbial prepositions. In addition, improper prepositions are never prefixed to verbs. *See also* proper preposition.

inceptive. *adj.* Giving emphasis to the beginning of the verbal action (Lat. *inceptivus*, "starting"). This term often appears in connection with aorist (see 2 Cor 8:9) or imperfect-tense verbs (see Mt 3:5). Also called inchoative, incipient or *ingressive.

inchoative. *See* inceptive.

incipient. *See* inceptive.

inclusio. *n.* A literary framing device in which the same word or phrase stands at the beginning and the end of a section. Sometimes called *bracketing.

inclusive language. *n.* Language that seeks to include previously excluded groups such as women and minorities, as in the substitution of *humankind* for *mankind*.

incommodi. Lat. "disadvantage." *See* dative of disadvantage.

indeclinable. *adj.* Of certain words, not belonging to a *declension; having no inflected forms (*see* inflection). These include conjunctions,*particles, prepositions and many proper names and place names. Sometimes a more precise definition is intended for verbs; indeclinable verbs are those which do not have number.

indefinite. *adj.* Not referring to a particular person or thing.

indefinite article. *n.* An article that does not particularize the substantive or clause it is modifying. In English, the definite article is *the* as opposed to the indefinite article *a* or *an*. Greek has only the one article.

indefinite plural. *n.* The third-person plural indicating no one in particular but "someone" in general.

indefinite pronoun. *n.* A pronoun used with an unknown or unspecified *antecedent, as in *someone* or *something*.

indefinite subject. *n.* The stated or implied subject *one* or *they*.

independent clause. *n.* A clause that can stand alone. Also referred to as an unrestricted clause or a main clause. *See* main clause.

independent infinitive. *n.* An infinitive that functions as the *main verb. See Romans 12:15.

independent participle. *n.* A participle that functions as the *main verb. Also known as the unrestricted participle. See Romans 12:9.

indicative. *n.* The mood that presents the verbal idea as being actual or real, as opposed to that which is only possible or intended (Lat. *indicativus*, "stating").

indirect attraction. *See* inverse attraction.

indirect command. *n.* A command that is not reproduced in the wording of the original statement but changed into the words of the reporter (e.g., Lk 18:40). *See also* indirect discourse.

indirect discourse. *n.* The reporting of what someone said by changing the wording of the original statement into the words of the reporter. For example, "Tom said he liked the symphony," as opposed to "Tom said, 'I like the symphony.'" The New Testament writers, by and large, prefer *direct discourse to indirect discourse. Also called reported speech or *oratio obliqua*.

indirect middle. *n.* The use of the middle voice to indicate that the *subject acts with self-interest.

indirect object. *n.* The part of speech that is indirectly affected by the verbal action. In Greek, the dative case generally marks the indirect object. In English, the indirect object is often marked by *to* or *for*.

indirect question. *n.* A question that is not reproduced in the wording of the original statement but changed into the words of the reporter. *See also* indirect discourse.

indirect quotation. *n.* A quotation that is not reproduced in the wording of the original statement but changed into the words of the reporter. *See also* indirect discourse.

indirect reflexive. *See* indirect middle.

indirect speech. *See* indirect discourse.

Indo-European. *adj.* Of a family of languages including most of the languages of Europe, the Indian subcontinent and regions in between. Sanskrit, Latin, Russian, German, English and *Greek are Indo-European languages.

inferential. *adj.* Denoting a deduction or a logical conclusion. —*n.* A conjunction or particle that signifies a deduction.

infinitive. *n.* An *indeclinable verbal form that has characteristics of a verb while also functioning like a *substantive; a "verbal noun."

infix. *n.* An *affix inserted into the middle of a word, within a *root or *stem. Infixing proper occurs in Semitic languages but not in Greek. In Greek, the tense formative of the first aorist, the so-called "infixed" sigma, appears between the verbal stem and the personal ending.

inflect. *v.* To alter a word (or be altered) by *inflection.

inflected language. *n.* A language in which words typically contain more than one *morpheme and in which various *grammatical functions and relations are indicated through *inflections. Also known as a fusional language.

inflection. *n.* Change in the *form of a word—especially substantives and adjectives—to express *grammatical meanings such as case, number and tense.

inflectional morphology. *See* morphology.

ingressive. *adj.* Giving emphasis to the *beginning* of the verbal action. This term usually appears in conjunction with aorist tense verbs; sometimes they denote an action starting. Also called inceptive or inchoative. See Romans 6:13; 1 Peter 5:8.

innerbiblical exegesis. In gospel criticism, the study of how texts have been reused, reinterpreted, and reapplied within the text itself by authors and redactors.

inscription. *n.* Writing that is marked, carved or engraved, often on stone, wood or metal.

instantaneous present. *n.* A present-tense verb that denotes action that occurs at a moment in time. Also called aoristic present and punctiliar present. See Mark 2:5; Acts 16:18.

instrumental. *adj.* Denoting agency, means or cause. The term is used of datives and prepositions. It is a separate *case in the *eight-case system.

instrumental dative. *See* dative of instrument/means.

intensive. *adj.* Tending to emphasize or intensify. A number of elements can function in this way, especially particles and pronouns. The term also describes certain tense usage, as in the *intensive perfect, which denotes a perfect-tense verb that emphasizes the result of the verbal action (also called resultative).

intensive middle. *See* indirect middle.

intensive perfect. *n.* A perfect-tense verb that functions as an emphatic present. Some grammars use this terminology to describe a perfect that emphasizes the result of the verbal action.

intensive pronoun. *n.* The use of αὐτός as a *pronoun to emphasize the notion of identity, as in "Mark *himself* will fry the fish." When αὐτός is in the *attributive position, it serves to identify and is translated "same" (see 2 Cor 4:13); when it is in the *predicate position, it functions as a true intensifier, meaning "self" (see 1 Thess 4:16).

interdental. *adj.* Produced by inserting the tip of the tongue between the upper and lower teeth. —*n.* An interdental sound.

interjection. *n.* An exclamatory utterance that can stand alone grammatically and is often emotive (Lat. *interiectio*, "something thrown in"). See Galatians 3:1.

interlinear Bible. *n.* A book that presents the biblical text in the original language with a *translation (a *gloss) above or below each word. The term can also refer to a biblical text that has commentary between the lines.

interlingua. *See* lingua franca.

intermediate agency. *See* agency.

internal borrowing. *See* analogic change.

internal criticism. *n.* Interpretation of the biblical text with special emphasis on its internal elements (word order, level of Christology, etc.).

internal dative. *See* cognate dative.

internal evidence. *n.* The evidence pertaining to a particular *text-critical issue concerned with scribal habits and tendencies, as well as *intrinsic probability (i.e., the sense of the larger passage in which the issue is found: the author's *style, the flow of the argument, etc.).

internal object. *See* cognate accusative.

interpolation. *n.* In the process of copying, the insertion of material into a text; or the interpolated material itself.

interrogative. *adj.* Having the nature of a question. —*n.* A pronoun or particle that functions to mark a question.

interrogative indicative. *n.* The use of an indicative mood verb in a question.

interrogative pronoun. *n.* A pronoun used to ask a question.

intertextuality. *n.* The mutual relationship among texts. Or, more precisely, the repetition, interweaving or reworking of biblical texts, ideas or *motifs; or the embedding of portions of or *allusions to one passage (called a *subtext) within another. Also referred to as *innerbiblical exegesis.

intervocalic. *adj.* Of consonant sounds, occurring between vowels. Such sounds often take on certain phonetic characteristics or behave peculiarly. An intervocalic sigma is often dropped and the remaining vowels contract.

intransitive. *adj.* Of verbs, not requiring a *direct object. E.g., in the sentence "Heather ran," the verb needs no direct object to complete the sense. On the other hand, a *transitive verb must have a direct object, as in "Abner tormented Zoe."

intransitive sentence. *n.* A sentence with an intransitive verb as its main verb.

intrinsic evidence. *n.* Evidence for a *text-critical issue pertaining to an author's *style, vocabulary and argument.

intrinsic probability. *n.* The likelihood of a variant based on the *original author's *style, vocabulary or argument.

introductory formula. *See* formula.

invention. *n.* In rhetoric, the discovery of the resources for argumentation and persuasion thought to be intrinsic to a given rhetorical problem.

inventory of sounds. *n.* The phonetic segments of a language.

inverse attraction. *n.* The transfer (or attraction) of the *case of a *relative pronoun to its *antecedent. Normally relative pronouns take the gender and number of their antecedent, while their case is determined by their function in their clause. Thus very often relative pronouns and their antecedents do not share the same case. Their close connection, however, explains why sometimes they react to one another. When inverse attraction occurs the antecedent is influenced by the presence of the relative pronoun and takes on its case. On the other hand, attraction of the case of the antecedent to the relative (termed simply *attraction) is much more common.

inverted parallelism. *See* chiasm.

Ionic Greek. *n.* One of the *dialects of classical Greek, which is found in Homer, Herodotus and others.

iota adscript. *n.* The letter iota written alongside the other letters, as opposed to *iota subscript, under the line.

iota subscript. *n.* A subscripted iota written under a vowel (ῳ), which has no effect on the pronunciation of the word.

iotacism. *See* itacism.

ipsissima verba. Lat. "the very words." —*n.* A verbatim quotation. The expression is usually used in Gospel studies. The handful of *Aramaic utterances attributed to Jesus in the Gospels (e.g., *"Talitha cum,"* Mk 5:41) seem to be examples of *ipsissima verba.* Sometimes referred to as *ipsissima verba Jesu. See also ipsissima vox.*

ipsissima vox. Lat. "the very voice." —*n.* A restatement that captures the precise meaning. The expression is used in Gospel studies to indicate that while a Gospel saying may not record the words of Jesus verbatim (**ipsissima verba*), it nevertheless renders his message accurately.

irony. *n.* A humorous or sarcastic statement intended to convey the opposite of its *literal meaning (εἰρωνεία, "pretense"), as in "Mike is a smart dresser, especially the mismatched socks." Also called *antiphrasis. See 2 Corinthians 11:19-20.

irregular. *adj.* Not conforming to rule. Verbs that are termed irregular do not *decline according to the normal pattern.

isocolon. *n.* A sequence of two or more *coordinate clauses that consist of similar constructions and a similar number of words or syllables. See Romans 3:25b-26a.

isogloss. *n.* The boundary separating one regional *dialect from another.

isomorphic. *adj.* Having one-to-one correspondence. The term was originally used in linguistics of grammatical structures or the constituent parts of a discourse, but it can also refer to other language features.

itacism. *n.* The drift in vowel pronunciation toward the sound of iota (ι) in *Hellenistic Greek. Also called iotacism. In textual criticism, it refers to errors arising in transmission in which two similar sounding words were confused, often involving iota, but not exclusively.

Itala. *See* Old Latin.

iterative. *adj.* Characterized by repetition, continuity or verbal action occurring at intervals. Also called frequentative.

J

jargon. *n.* The special vocabulary of the members of a profession or other group.

Jerusalem Talmud. *See* Palestinian Talmud. *See also* Gemara.

Johannine. *adj.* Of or relating to John or the writings attributed to John, i.e., the Gospel of John, 1, 2 and 3 John, Revelation.

Johannine comma. *n.* The interpolated passage 1 John 5:7-8, absent from the early manuscripts, the Greek fathers and the ancient *versions, and problematic elsewhere. It may have originated as a marginal *gloss.

Josephus, Flavius. *prop. n.* A first-century Jew who was appointed by the emperor Vespasian to serve as court historian. His works *The Jewish War* and *The Antiquities of the Jews* provide important historical background material for the New Testament. —*n.* Shorthand for the writings of Josephus.

K

Kaige recension. *n.* A *version of the Old Testament in Greek that was either translated directly from the original languages or was a revision of an earlier Greek translation. The name comes from its unusual use of καίγε. It is in the same text tradition as *Theodotion; also called the proto-Theodotion recension.

kappa aorist. *n.* A verb that uses -κα to form the aorist tense, as in the *athematic conjugation (μι verbs).

kephalaia. *pl. n.* Chapter divisions, which were regularly incorporated into manuscripts. Also called capitulation. *See also* Eusebian Canons.

kerygma. *n.* The apostolic message of the gospel; or the act of preaching the gospel (κήρυγμα, "proclamation"). The term often refers to the message as it was first proclaimed, presumably as in the sermons in Acts and elsewhere (e.g., 1 Cor 15:1-4; Gal 1:3-4; 3:1b; 1 Thess 1:10).

Khirbet Qumran. *See* Dead Sea Scrolls.

Kleinliteratur. Germ. "low [or light] literature." —*n.* Works derived from popular storytelling, as opposed to formal *literary works (*Hochliteratur*).

Koine. *n.* The Greek language as it was spoken when the Mediterranean world was Hellenized (*see* Hellenic period). (Κοινή is the fem. adj. of κοινός, "common," implying διάλεκτος.) The convergence of cultures and the commingling of Greek *dialects produced a type of Greek that lost some of the subtleties of classical Greek and that was less "refined" than *literary Greek during the same period. The term is used interchangeably with *Hellenistic Greek.

Koine Text. *See* Byzantine text-type.

Kompositionsgeschichte. Germ. "composition criticism." *See* redaction criticism.

Kunstprosa. Germ. "artistic prose." —*n.* Writing that achieves an overall pleasing effect.

L

L. *n.* A hypothetical source that evidently stands behind Luke's unique material; or the material itself. *See also* Four-Source hypothesis.

labial. *adj.* Of speech sounds, articulated with the lips. —*n.* A labial speech sound.

labiodental. *adj.* Of speech sounds, produced by touching the bottom lip to the upper teeth. —*n.* A labiodental speech sound (e.g., "f" and "v").

lacuna. *n.* A damaged or missing part of a manuscript (Lat. "hole"). *pl.* lacunae.

laryngeal. *n.* A speech sound articulated in the larynx.

Lasterkatalog. Germ. "catalog of vices." *See* vice list, ethical list and *Tugendkatalog.*

Latinism. *n.* A word, idiom or grammatical construction derived from Latin.

Leben-Jesu Forschung. Germ. "Life of Jesus research."

lectio brevior. Lat. "*shorter reading."

lectio brevior lectio potior. Lat. "the *shorter reading is the preferable reading."

lectio brevior potior. Lat. "the *shorter reading is preferable."

lectio difficilima. Lat. "the most difficult reading." *See* more difficult reading.

lectio difficilior. Lat. "*more difficult reading."

lectio difficilior lectio potior. Lat. "the *more difficult reading is the preferable reading."

lectio difficilior probabilior. Lat. "the *more difficult reading is more probable."

lectio facilior. Lat. "easier reading." *See* more difficult reading.

lectio marginalis. Lat. "reading in the margin." *See* gloss.

lectio potior. Lat. "preferable reading." *See* preferred reading.

lectio praeferenda est. Lat. "the *preferred reading is."

lectionary. *n.* A book containing portions of biblical passages (lections) for scheduled reading in worship according to the Christian calendar. In textual criticism, the term refers to ancient lectionaries.

lector. *n.* A person who reads aloud in order that multiple *copyists may work simultaneously.

legend. *n.* In *literary or *form criticism, a broad *genre category involving a religious or devotional story, often including exaltation of a hero.

lemma. *n.* In textual criticism, the biblical text as it appears in ancient commentary manuscripts, prior to the commentary itself; or the text in a *critical apparatus. In *lexicology, a word or phrase listed at the beginning of a dictionary entry; a headword. Or similarly, a heading or title in a text. In linguistics, the semantic and syntactic characteristics that a speaker attaches to a word.

lengthening. *n.* The shifting of short vowels to long vowels due to in-

flectional changes (*see* inflection). In the case of *compensatory lengthening, ε becomes ει and ο becomes ω; for *augmentation of a word-
initial vowel, ε becomes η and ο becomes ω. *See also* temporal augment.
Sometimes referred to as formative lengthening.

less probable future condition. *See* fourth class condition.

lesser to greater. *See a fortiori.*

lexeme. *n.* A minimal unit in the semantic system of a language; the
words listed in a lexicon (as opposed to all the grammatical variants
that the lexeme can produce (*buy* in relation to *buys, bought, buying,
buyer,* etc.).

lexical. *adj.* Pertaining to words and their meanings.

lexical entry. *See* lexical form.

lexical form. *n.* The *form of a word as it appears in the *lexicon. Older
Greek lexica and *grammars used the infinitive for verbs, but today
the first-person singular present active indicative is standard. The
nominative singular is the lexical form for nouns; for adjectives, the
masculine nominative singular. Also called the lexical entry.

lexical meaning. *n.* The meaning of a word conceived of separately from
a given context, i.e., apart from *syntax.

lexicography. *n.* The work of compiling or writing a dictionary or some
other similar language tool.

lexicology. *n.* The branch of language study concerned with the words
of a language and the development of valid methods of word study.

lexicon. *n.* A dictionary.

lexis. *n.* The vocabulary of a language. In rhetoric, the choice of words
and the way they are put together. Broadly conceived, it refers to an
author's *style. On a microlevel, lexis refers to the basic semantic range
of a particular word.

ligature. *n.* A stroke connecting two *cursive letters.

linear. *adj.* Pertaining to verbal action that is ongoing or progressive in
nature, as opposed to *punctiliar action, which occurs at a point in
time. The term can also be used to describe the force of nonverbal elements, such as εἰς or ἐπί with the accusative. Also called durative, ongoing or progressive. In *linguistics, the term can be used to refer to
the structuring of features in narrative.

lingua franca. *n.* A language that serves as a medium of communication
between diverse peoples. *Koine served this purpose until it became
so dominant that in many areas it was no longer just a secondary language. Originally the term referred to a hybrid of Italian, French,
Spanish, Arabic, Greek and Turkish spoken in the countries bordering

the eastern Mediterranean Sea (Ital. "Frankish language"). Also called an interlingua.

lingual. *n.* A speech sound articulated with the tongue.

linguist. *n.* A specialist in *linguistics.

linguistics. *n.* The scientific study of language. There are various forms, including *diachronic linguistics, the study of language change over time (also called historical linguistics or *philology); *synchronic linguistics, the study of language at a given point in time; comparative linguistics, which identifies common characteristics among languages; and applied linguistics, which can refer to language learning (and teaching) theory.

linking verb. *n.* The *copula.

lipography. *n.* In copying a text, the accidental omission of material when the eye jumps over several letters or words; or the end result of such an omission.

liquid. *n.* A speech sound that is made by a certain amount of obstruction of the airstream in the mouth but not so much that it cannot be prolonged like a vowel. The term specifically refers to λ and ρ, but liquid verbs include verbs whose *stems end in λ, ρ, μ and ν.

liquid aorist. *n.* A verb *stem whose final consonant is λ, μ, ν or ρ, causing it to behave differently in the formation of the aorist tense, i.e., it adds alpha (α) rather than sigma-alpha (σα).

liquid future. *n.* A verb *stem whose final consonant is λ, μ, ν or ρ, causing it to behave differently in the formation of the future tense, i.e., the usual sigma drops out and the remaining letters contract.

liquid verb. *n.* A verb *stem whose final consonant is λ, μ, ν or ρ.

literal. *adj.* Of language, presented or understood in its primary, matter-of-fact sense. Some definitions of "literal" are misleading—most are problematic—since a great deal of communication regarded as *nonliteral actually points to things that are very real and "literal."

literary. *adj.* Of or pertaining to words or writing; or, more specifically, appropriate to or pertaining to literature, as opposed to everyday writing or speech. *Literary Koine (also called literary Greek) refers to Greek used by writers (e.g., Plutarch) during the *Hellenistic period, but of a more sophisticated style.

literary aorist. *n.* An aorist tense verb that is past from the reader's point of view but actually present from the writer's point of view. Also called the *epistolary aorist. See Acts 23:30; Philippians 2:28.

literary criticism. *n.* The discipline concerned with the *literary characteristics of a text: its vocabulary, forms, structure, style, use of figures and devices, etc. Sometimes source criticism is subsumed as a component of literary criticism.

literary dependence. *n.* One writer's reliance on the written work of another, which gives rise to verbal agreement. The synoptic problem pertains to whether or not we can identify literary dependence among the Synoptic Gospels and the nature of that dependence.

literary device. *n.* A technique used in writing to achieve a particular effect. This refers primarily to *figures of speech in a rather formal sense (e.g., metonymy, metaphor, etc.), but also to any number of means of enriching ordinary communication.

literary Greek. *See* literary Koine.

literary Koine. *n.* The Greek language as it was used by certain writers during the *Hellenistic period (e.g., *Josephus, *Philo, Plutarch). It is differentiated from *Koine, the everyday Greek of the period, including the New Testament documents, because it is considered in some sense more sophisticated.

literary plural. *See* editorial *we*.

litotes. *n.* The negation of something in order to affirm the opposite; or understatement in order to give *emphasis (λιτότης, "simplicity"). E.g., "Sheryl's not a bad swimmer." Also called meiosis. See Acts 14:28; 15:2; 21:39; Romans 1:16.

Little Apocalypse. *n.* A reference to Mark 13, according to a theory that this passage originated independently as a Jewish-Christian tract written as a result of religious persecution and was later interpolated. *See also* apocalypse, apocalyptic.

loan translation. *n.* The phenomenon of one language *borrowing another word or expression by translating it literally. E.g., *skyscraper* entered French as *gratte-ciel* ("scrape-sky"), and German as *Wolkenkratzer* ("cloud-scrape").

loanword. *n.* A word adopted from one language into another and naturalized to some degree, as in *garage* or *hors d'oeuvre* (both French).

local text. *n.* A text form that is peculiar to a geographical location. Also referred to as a regional original.

local-genealogical method. *See* reasoned eclecticism.

locative. *adj.* or *n.* In the *eight-case system, the *case denoting location, sphere or destination, among other things. The eight-case system's dative instrumental and locative are subsumed under the *five-case system's dative.

locus classicus. Lat. *locus*, "place" + *classicus*, "belonging to the highest class." —*n.* A passage commonly cited as the best text in support of a particular doctrine or concept.

logia. *pl.* of logion.

logion. *n.* A succint saying of Jesus. The plural, logia, often refers to a hypothetical source or collection of sayings of Jesus, which is thought by some to have been a source for the *Evangelists. Papias (ca. 2nd cent.) wrote that Matthew had access to the logia of Jesus in Hebrew.

logos. *n.* As a rhetorical term dealing with theories of argument and persuasion, the content and logic of a speech. *See also* ethos and pathos.

long vowel. *n.* A vowel sound whose duration when uttered was originally longer relative to other vowels but now is differentiated solely on the basis of its quality (the sound produced as a result of the *manner of articulation).

lower criticism. *n.* A somewhat pejorative term that refers to *textual criticism, as opposed to the other types (form criticism, redaction criticism, etc.). The designation is no longer widely used.

Lucianic Text. *See* Byzantine text-type.

Luke's great omission. *n.* Assuming *Markan priority and *literary dependence, the name given to Mark 6:45—8:26, a large section that Luke omitted from his Gospel.

LXX. *See* Septuagint.

M

M. *n.* A hypothetical source that evidently stands behind Matthew's unique material; or the material itself. *See also* Four-Source hypothesis.

macrocontext. *n.* The larger literary setting of a passage above the paragraph level, with special reference to the place and function of the passage within the entire work.

macrostructure. *n.* The larger units of speech and writing—anything above the sentence level. *See also* discourse analysis.

main clause. *n.* The clause that contains the *main verb and to which, in a *compound sentence, other clauses are subordinate. As such, it can stand alone—it is not *dependent on or subordinate to another clause. Also referred to as the independent or principal clause.

main verb. *n.* The principal verb in a clause to which other verbal elements are subordinate. It is normally a *finite verb. Also called the controlling verb.

Majority Text. *See* Byzantine text-type.

majority text method. *n.* An approach to textual criticism that essentially excludes any appeal to *internal evidence but rather argues that *readings represented by a majority of manuscripts are original.

majuscule. *n.* A capital letter; or a *manuscript composed in capital letters.

makarism. *n.* A beatitude or blessing (μακάριος, "blessed"); a form-critical category of this type.

manner of articulation. *n.* The type of processes involved in pronouncing speech sounds, which provides one of the main parameters in their classification.

manner participle. *n.* An adverbial participle that indicates the manner in which the action of the main verb is accomplished. Also known as modal participle.

manuscript. *n.* In textual criticism, a handwritten document. There are now extant, in whole or in part, approximately 5,300 Greek New Testament manuscripts.

Marcionite prologues. *pl. n.* Material found in a number of Latin *Vulgate manuscripts, which provides, for Paul's letters, brief descriptions of the addressees and reasons for writing, with stress on Paul's conflict with false apostles.

Markan priority. *n.* The notion that the Gospel of Mark was written before Matthew and Luke. Almost always accompanying this inference is the belief that Mark provided the basis for one or both of the other *Synoptic Gospels. *See also* synoptic problem.

marker. *See* function word.

masculine. *adj.* Designating one of three *genders in Greek (the others being feminine and neuter). —*n.* A masculine word. Since Greek for the most part follows *grammatical gender rather than *natural gender, there is rarely any discernible explanation for why a word is a particular gender.

mass noun. *n.* A noun that cannot be pluralized because its referent is considered inseparable (having no clear or natural bounds) and uncountable. Also referred to as noncount or uncountable nouns.

meaning shift. *n.* Semantic change in which the meaning of a word changes over time.

mechanical layout. *See* grammatical analysis.

medial. *adj.* Occurring in the middle. For example, a medial vowel is any vowel that is not *word-initial or *word-final.

meiosis. *n.* Understatement (μείωσις, "lessening"). *See* litotes. See Matthew 15:26; Hebrews 9:12.

merism. *n.* The juxtaposition of two elements that represent two extremes in order to suggest everything in between, as in "I've read Irving's first novel; I've read his most recent novel," or "In the beginning

God created the heavens and the earth" (Gen 1:1). Also referred to as enumeratio. Also merismus.

merismus. *See* merism.

metabasis. *n.* In rhetoric, an abrupt change of subject or a return to the main subject after a digression. See Philippians 3:2.

metaclisis. *n.* Repetition of the same word, *inflected differently, anywhere but at the beginnings of successive clauses. See 1 Corinthians 9:20.

metalanguage. *n.* Language used to describe an object of study. In linguistics, the terminology used to discuss language.

metanarrative. *n.* That which in some sense exists above the text in the consciousness of the reader.

metaphor. *n.* A *figure of speech in which an aspect of one thing is pointed out by implicitly comparing it with something else or by simply identifying it as the thing to which it is being compared, as in "the autumn of life" or "Dave is a rock" (μεταφορά, "a transference"). See Galatians 4:21-31.

metaphrase. *n.* A word-for-word translation. —*v.* To subtly alter the meaning of a text.

metaplasm. *n.* The alteration of a word by the addition, subtraction or transposition of letters. Sometimes used synonymously with *heteroclisis.

metathesis. *n.* In the process of copying the biblical text, the transposition of letters, words or whole phrases (see Mk 14:65). The term can also be used of *phonological processes in which sequential sounds are transposed.

metonymy. *n.* A *figure of speech in which one thing is designated by the mention of something associated with it (μετωνυμία, "a change of name"), as in "The White House denied the allegations," which uses *White House* to mean the president or his staff. See Romans 5:9; Colossians 1:16; 4:18.

μι verb. *See* athematic conjugation.

microcontext. *n.* The smaller *literary setting of a passage of text (anything below the paragraph level).

microstructure. *n.* The smaller units of speech and writing—anything up to the sentence level.

middle voice. *adj.* or *n.* The voice that denotes verbal action in which the *subject is being affected by its own action or is acting upon itself.

midrash. *n.* Jewish/rabbinic biblical interpretation; a specific exegetical comment; or a *genre of such (*pl.* midrashim). Halakic midrashim pertains to legal matters; haggadic midrashim pertains to nonlegal matters.

mimesis. *n.* Literature that is imitative of nature, life and so on. — *adj.* Mimetic.

minimal pair. *n.* In *phonology, two words that differ by only one sound (e.g., *mine* and *nine*).

minuscule. *n.* Cursive script; or a manuscript written in this style. —*adj.* Designating this style. Minuscule script became the norm for manuscript production after the ninth century, whereupon these manuscripts grew to outnumber *uncial manuscripts ten to one. Minuscules are designated by Arabic numerals without a zero preceding (e.g., 1739). Also referred to as a running hand.

Mishnah. *n.* A collection of traditional Jewish halakic (legal) material compiled early in the third century A.D. It is divided into six major divisions (orders) and sixty-three tractates. Also Mishna.

modal. *adj.* Of verbs, pertaining to *mood; of particles, denoting manner or mood (sometimes means). For example, particles will often enhance the modal character of a sentence: ἄν with the subjunctive gives more prominence to the idea inherent in the subjunctive; the interrogative particles clarify or enhance the notion of inquiry, etc. The term is also used to denote *attendant circumstance.

modal participle. *See* manner participle.

mode. Synonymous with *mood.

moderate eclecticism. *See* reasoned eclecticism.

modern Greek. *n.* The Greek language spoken in the present; or more broadly, Greek from A.D. 1450 to the present.

modification. *See* modify.

modifier. *n.* A word or clause that describes, qualifies or limits another word or clause.

modify. *v.* To qualify, delimit or specify the meaning of. Adjectives, adverbs and dependent grammatical elements functioning like either of these are said to modify other elements.

monadic article. *n.* The use of the *article to identify someone or something that is unique (μόνος, "by itself").

monograph. *n.* A scholarly essay or book, usually quite limited in scope.

monolectic. *adj.* Of Greek verbs, denoting their ability to contain sufficient grammatical information (i.e., mood, voice and aspect) to constitute complete clauses.

monomorphemic. *adj.* Consisting of one *morpheme. —*n.* A monomorphemic word.

monophthong. *n.* A vowel that is pronounced with no change in sound quality. This is in contrast with *diphthongs, which contain a *glide.

monosyllabic. *adj.* Having just one syllable. —*n.* A monosyllabic word.

mood. *n.* The feature of the Greek verbal system that denotes the nature of the verbal idea with regard to its actuality or potentiality. The moods are the *imperative, *indicative, *optative and *subjunctive.

more difficult reading. *n.* In textual criticism, the more difficult variant among the various *readings for a particular textual critical issue, because it seems awkward, uncharacteristic or more difficult to explain. The more difficult or harder reading is often thought to be the original reading since *scribes tended to smooth out difficulties (*see lectio difficilior probabilior*).

more probable future condition. *See* third class condition.

morpheme. *n.* A minimal grammatical element of a language, including free forms (morphemes that can appear as words) and bound forms (mainly *affixes). *See also* free morpheme, bound morpheme.

morphological. *adj.* Of or pertaining to morphology or to the forms of words.

morphology. *n.* The study of the structure of words and the system of *forms of a language. Derivational morphology pertains to the formation of words; inflectional morphology involves the study of *inflections. Sometimes *phonology is conceived of as a subcategory of morphology.

motif. *n.* A recurrent, pervasive or dominant element in an artistic or *literary work.

movable consonants. *n.* A consonant that may or may not appear at the end of a word and that does not affect meaning. *Movable nu (ν) is the most prominent in Greek.

movable nu. *n.* A nu (ν) that is placed after a word-final vowel when the following word begins with a vowel. Actually, this was the rule in classical Greek, but in the New Testament it often appears even before consonants. The presence or absence of a movable nu does not affect meaning.

multiplicative. *adj.* Denoting multiplication or quantity (see ἐπί in Phil 2:27); or words formed with the *suffixes -πλοῦς (see Lk 19:8) and -πλασίων with numerals (see Mt 19:29; Mk 10:30; Lk 8:8; 18:30).

myth. *n.* In biblical criticism, literary forms that speak of the transcendent, the world beyond, in this-worldly terms. Also myth provides commentary on human experience and an ethical message or a word about salvation.

N

Nag Hammadi Library. *n.* An extensive collection of mostly Gnostic documents dating from the fourth century A.D. The codices (*see* codex), written in *Coptic, were discovered in upper (Southern) Egypt in the mid 1940s.

narratee. *n.* In reader-oriented criticism, the hypothetical respondent to a text.

narratio. *n.* In rhetoric, the statement of the facts, which follows the *prologue (*exordium). *See also* rhetorical criticism.

narrative criticism. *n.* The discipline concerned with interpreting the biblical text, particularly narrative, as a literary production, with emphasis on features such as plot, structure, the ordering of events, characterization and other literary techniques. Also called narratological criticism.

narratological criticism. *See* narrative criticism.

narratology. *n.* The study of narrative texts, especially the structural elements.

narrowing. *n.* Semantic change in which the meaning of a word changes over time to become less extensive. The opposite of *broadening.

nasal. *adj.* Denoting a speech sound produced by complete closure of the mouth so that audible air escapes through the nose. —*n.* A nasal sound.

nasal gamma. *See* gamma nasal.

natural class. *n.* A class of sounds characterized by a phonetic feature (*see* phoneme) that pertains to all members of the set.

natural gender. *n.* In certain languages, the phenomenon of words taking on the gender of the persons or things they represent, as when the word *father* (ὁ πατήρ) is masculine. For the most part, Greek does not follow natural gender (pronouns are the exception) but rather *grammatical gender. Also called sense gender.

near demonstrative. *n.* A *demonstrative pronoun that functions to specify that the substantive it refers to is near to the speaker/writer, e.g., *this* and *these. See also* far demonstative.

negative. *adj.* Pertaining to negation. —*n.* A word that functions to negate a *clause.

Nestle-Aland. *n.* A Greek New Testament, in several editions, named after its primary editors, including in its apparatus a wider range of textual variants than those listed in the *UBS text, but with less evidence (fewer manuscripts) for each. The Greek text is identical to the

UBS text and provides the text base for most modern English translations except the NKJV.

neuter. *adj.* Designating one of three *genders in Greek (the others being masculine and feminine). —*n.* A neuter word. Since Greek for the most part follows *grammatical gender rather than *natural gender, there is rarely any discernible explanation for why a word is a particular gender.

Neutral text-type. *See* Alexandrian text-type.

neutralization rules. *pl. n.* Phonological rules that obliterate the contrast between two speech sounds in certain environments.

New Criticism. *n.* An approach to the biblical text that rejects "extrinsic" factors bearing upon its meaning—biographical, sociological, philosophical, even the author's intention—rather, form and content are inseparable; the focus is on the text itself as a literary artifact, with emphasis on stable meaning and structural characteristics. New Criticism is usually associated with *structuralism, *formalism and *literary or *rhetorical criticism.

New Testament Pseudepigrapha. *n.* The large collection of pseudonymous *gospels, books of acts, *epistles and *apocalypses that were not recognized by the church and thus not included in the New Testament *canon. Sometimes used synonymously with New Testament *Apocrypha. *See also* pseudonym, pseudonymity.

nomen rectum. *n.* The *genitive that is governed by a *substantive, the *nomen regens.* Sometimes simply referred to as the genitive *noun.

nomen regens. *n.* The *substantive that governs the *genitive, the *nomen rectum.* The *nomen regens* can also be represented by the article or a pronoun. Also called the *head noun.

nomen sacrum. Lat. "sacred name." *See nomina sacra.*

nomina sacra. *pl. n.* Frequently occurring "sacred names" in the biblical text (e.g., Θεός, Χριστός) that were abbreviated by writing only a portion of their letters along with a horizontal line above them to let the reader know of their existence.

nominal. *adj.* Of, pertaining to or functioning as a *noun or *pronoun, or to a name.

nominative. *adj.* or *n.* The *case that normally functions to indicate the grammatical *subject of a clause.

nominative absolute. *n.* A grammatically independent nominative word or phrase. See 1 Corinthians 1:1; Revelation 1:1.

nominative for vocative. *n.* The use of a nominative case substantive in the place of a *vocative. See Matthew 16:17; Luke 8:54.

nominative of appellation. *n.* The use of a nominative case substantive for a title, which functions as though it were a proper name. See John 13:13; Revelation 9:11.

nominative of exclamation. *n.* The use of an absolute nominative-case substantive in an exclamation or *interjection. See Mark 3:34; Romans 7:24.

nominativus pendens. See pendent nominative.

noncanonical. *adj.* Of writings or books that were not accepted into the biblical *canon. Also called extracanonical.

noncount noun. *See* mass noun.

nonfactive. *See* factive.

nonfinite verb. *n.* A verb that is not finite, i.e., *participles and *infinitives. *See also* finite verb.

nonliteral. *adj.* Of language, presented or understood in some sense other than its primary, matter-of-fact sense. *See also* literal.

nonobstruents. *See* sonorant.

nonrestrictive. *adj.* Of modifying words and phrases, nonessential to the identity of the *head noun.

nonsense reading. *n.* In textual criticism, a *reading that is nonsensical because it is *ungrammatical or consists of an impossible lexical form, or because in any other way it lacks recognizable meaning.

nonthematic. *See* athematic.

noun. *n.* A word that represents a person, place, thing, quality, state or action and that can function as the *subject or *object of a *verb.

noun phrase. *n.* A noun with all its *modifying words and *phrases.

number. *n.* The feature of a word whereby its singularity or plurality is indicated—whether it refers to one or more persons or things.

Nunc Dimittis. n. The prayer of Simeon in Luke 2:29-32, so named because of the first words of the Latin text, *"Nunc dimittis servum tuum."*

O

object. *n.* A substantive that either receives the action of a verb or participle, or is governed by a preposition.

object complement construction. *n.* A construction in which a verb takes two accusatives: one functions as the *direct object, the other *complements the *object. Also referred to as the double accusative. See John 15:15; Romans 6:11; 10:9.

objective case. *See* oblique case.

objective genitive. *n.* A genitive substantive that functions as the direct object (i.e., it receives the action) of the verbal idea implied in the *head noun. E.g., ζῆλον θεοῦ ("zeal for God," Rom 10:2); also Romans 3:22; 1 Corinthians 1:6.

oblique case. *n.* Any case other than the *nominative or *vocative. These are sometimes referred to as the objective cases since they can function to denote the *object of a verb. The term oblique is also used occasionally to designate any mood other than the *indicative. Also referred to as the direct cases.

oblique optative. *n.* The use of the *optative in *indirect questions after a *secondary tense. See Luke 1:29; 8:9.

obstruent. *n.* A class of speech sounds that includes nonnasal *stops, *fricatives and *affricates.

occasion. *n.* The situation that gave rise to the composition of a particular biblical book; the events surrounding its production.

occasional. *adj.* Of biblical books, arising as a response to a particular need; ad hoc. E.g., Paul's occasional letters were triggered by particular events.

octavo. *n.* A sheet folded three times and cut to make a total of eight leaves or sixteen pages. Or a book made of such pages. *See also* folio and quarto.

ode. *n.* A poem or song, as in Ephesians 5:19 and Colossians 3:16.

Old Greek. *n.* The earliest pre-Christian translations of the Hebrew Bible into Greek. Also called the proto-Septuagint (or proto-LXX; *see* Septuagint).

Old Latin. *pl. n.* Designation for New Testament *manuscripts in Latin that are independent of the *Vulgate (some of which antedate the Vulgate, which was completed in A.D. 405). The traditional siglum for these manuscripts is *it*, which stands for "Itala"; they are represented in critical texts by lower-case letters.

Old Testament Pseudepigrapha. *n.* The large, diverse collection of Jewish and Hellenistic Jewish writings that predate the New Testament and were not included in the Old Testament *canon or in the *Apocrypha.

omega verbs. *See* thematic conjugation.

omnitemporal. *See* gnomic.

onomasticon. *n.* A *lexicon of names (especially proper names); or, more narrowly, philological aids that purport to provide the meaning and *etymology of proper names. *pl.* onomastica.

onomatopoeia. *n.* The use of words that are derived from natural sounds, such as *buzz* or *oink* (ὀνοματοποιία, "making a name").

open vowel. *n.* A vowel sound that is pronounced with the mouth more open than closed.

open-class words. *pl. n.* A category of words that have *lexical content; a class of words to which new words are commonly added. *See also* closed-class words.

opening vowel. *n.* A vowel that begins a word. *See also* word-initial.

opisthograph. *n.* A manuscript that has writing on the back or on both sides. See Revelation 5:1.

optative. *adj.* The *mood used in prayers, wishes and other instances to denote verbal action that is possible. —*n.* A word in the optative.

optative of obtainable wish. *See* voluntative optative.

oral sound. *n.* A speech sound in which air escapes through the mouth, in contrast to a *nasal sound in which it does not.

oral tradition. *n.* The handing down of unwritten stories and sayings; or the body of material itself. The term is used in New Testament *criticism primarily of Gospel stories or sayings.

oratio obliqua. Lat. "*indirect discourse."

oratio recta. Lat. "straight discourse." *See* direct discourse.

ordinal number. *n.* A number used to indicate order or position (first, second, third, etc.), as opposed to a *cardinal number, which indicates quantity (one, two, three, etc.).

Ordinary Gloss. *See Glossa Ordinaria*

original. *adj.* or *n.* Not derived, but first; authentic. The term is used to refer both to the *autographa (the original biblical documents no longer *extant) as well as to a particular variant in the manuscripts when one or more *correctors has changed the first copy (i.e., the original *hand, the second hand, etc.).

orismus. *n.* In rhetoric, furnishing a definition of a word to support one's argument or giving a certain action, behavior or event a name. See Romans 4:4.

orthography. *n.* The aspect of language study concerned with spelling, the arrangement of letters to represent spoken speech.

ostraca. *pl. n.* Pottery fragments (potsherds), which were used as writing material. Also ostracon. Some portions of the New Testament are preserved on ostraca.

otiose. *adj.* Of certain words and grammatical units, superfluous; lacking effect. *See also* circumlocution and pleonasm.

Oxford hypothesis. *n.* A proposed solution to the *synoptic problem that suggests that Mark was written first; and then Matthew and Luke, independently of one another, both used Mark and *Q, as well as other source material termed *M and *L respectively. Also known as the *Four-Source hypothesis. A variation of this is the *Two-Source hypothesis, which downplays or dismisses the role of Matthew's and Luke's exclusive sources.

oxymoron. *n.* A compact rhetorical device involving paradoxical elements. See Romans 6:8.

Oxyrhynchus papyri. *n.* A large number (several thousand) of *papyrus fragments, predominantly from the third and fourth centuries, found at Oxyrhynchus (also known as Behnesa) in northern Egypt.

oxytone. *n.* A word having an *acute accent on the ultima, its last syllable. *See also* barytone, paroxytone and proparoxytone.

P

palatal. *n.* A speech sound articulated with the tongue raised to the hard palate, as in the "sh" sound in English.

paleography. *n.* The study of ancient writing and documents, including determining the date of ancient texts.

Palestinian Talmud. *n.* The *Mishnah plus the Palestinian *Gemara (*commentary). Also known as Yerushalmi or Jerusalem Talmud. *See also* Babylonian Talmud.

palimpsest. *n.* A reused *parchment, after the original text has been scraped off (πάλιν, "again" + ψάω, "I scrape"). Using various methods, paleographers are often able to read the original text(s).

papyri. Plural of *papyrus.

papyrus. *n.* A writing material made from the plant by the same name. The fibrous pith inside the stem of the plant was cut open and laid flat. For added strength two layers of papyrus were pressed together with their fibers running perpendicular to one another. In some usage the term includes texts not only written on papyrus but also *ostraca, etc.

parable. *n.* A short instructive story that contains an analogy.

parablepsis. *n.* In copying a manuscript, the jumping of the eyes from one letter or *cluster of letters to a similar looking line, which causes unintentional errors in *transmission. Or the result, the error itself.

paradigm. *n.* A set of *inflected forms that illustrates a particular conjugational pattern (*see* conjugation) or *declension. In *form criticism, a brief narrative that grew out of early Christian preaching (*see* apothegm). In linguistics, paradigmatic relations refers to the set of substitutive relationships that a linguistic unit (a letter, a word, etc.) has with other units in a specific context.

paradosis. *n.* Traditional material; that which is handed down (παράδοσις, "tradition").

paradox. *n.* A rhetorical feature involving a statement that is or seems self-contradictory or contrary to reason. See Matthew 5:3-12; Mark 8:35; Luke 18:14; 1 Corinthians 1:25; 7:22; 2 Corinthians 4:8-11; 6:8-10; 12:10; Philippians 3:7.

paraenesis. *n.* Biblical material that involves instruction, exhortation or commands. Also paranesis or parenesis. — *adj.* *Paraenetic/parenetic.

paraenetic. *adj.* Pertaining to instruction, exhortation or command.

paragraph. *n.* A unit of writing, usually more than one *sentence, that speaks of a single theme and is somehow distinct from the material surrounding it.

paralipsis. *n.* A rhetorical device in which a comment is made about something by the suggestion that it will not be mentioned or does not need to be spoken of. Examples in English include the expressions "not to mention," and "to say nothing of." See 2 Corinthians 9:4; Philemon 19; Hebrews 11:32. Also paraleipsis/paralepsis. Also referred to as *apophasis.

parallel. *adj.* or *n.* Of a text that resembles another in terms of *lexical similarity, *literary quality or subject matter.

paranesis. *See* paraenesis.

paraphrase. *n.* A rewording or *translation that conveys the sense of the original but is not necessarily a word-for-word rendering. —*v.* Restate.

paratactic. *adj. See* parataxis.

parataxis. *n.* The linking of *clauses or *phrases together without utilizing *conjunctions that mark subordinate relationships. The opposite of *hypotaxis. The term can also be used when conjunctions are present (including an excessive use of καί), but *subordination of thought is downplayed. Paratactic style is characteristic of Semitic languages. Also called prostaxis. *See also* asyndeton. See Mark 14:37. Sometimes used of seemingly unrelated passages set in close proximity.

parchment. *n.* A prepared animal skin used for writing or drawing. The word is derived from the name of the ancient city Pergamum, where ostensibly the material was easy to come by. It is synonymous with *vellum, although this latter term denotes a higher quality material.

parechesis. *n.* *Assonance involving different words, as opposed to *cognates. See Luke 21:11; Hebrews 5:8; Romans 1:29, 31. *See also* annominatio and paronomasia.

parenesis. *See* paraenesis.

parent. *n.* In textual criticism, a manuscript that served as the model for another manuscript or manuscripts. In *philology, a parent language refers to an earlier form of a language.

parenthesis. *n.* A grammatically independent unit—usually a short phrase—placed in the middle of a sentence. See Romans 1:13; Galatians 2:6-7.

parenthetic nominative. *n.* A use of the nominative case to indicate the subject of an explanatory clause that is embedded within another clause. See Matthew 24:15; John 1:6; Revelation 2:9.

paronomasia. *n.* A play on words involving the repetition of similar-sounding words or the same word with different senses; punning. *See also* annominatio. See Luke 21:11; Romans 2:1; 2 Corinthians 9:8; Philippians 3:2-3; Hebrews 5:8.

paronym. *n.* A word that shares the same *root with another; a *cognate, as in *thermal* and *thermometer*.

paronymous. *adj.* Of words, sharing the same *root.

parousia. *n.* Advent. The term is used to speak of the promised return of Christ (see 1 Cor 15:23). The word is a *transliteration of παρουσία, which means "presence" or "arrival." The phrase "apostolic parousia" refers to Paul's writing about his future arrival at a church.

paroxytone. *n.* A word having an *acute accent on the penult, its next-to-last syllable. *See also* barytone, oxytone and proparoxytone.

parrhesia. *n.* Intentional (and perhaps contrived) refusal to mince words that seems to risk getting a negative reaction from an audience but instead gains rapport for the speaker/writer. See Romans 9:1.

parse. *v.* To identify the morphological characteristics of a word—its *form—and thus its syntactical function (Lat. *pars*, "part"). Some *grammars use the word *conjugate* in this sense, especially with verbs.

parsing guide. *n.* A book that lists words in their inflected *forms (*see* inflection) along with parsing information (*see* parse). The material can be arranged either alphabetically or canonically. Similar to an *analytical lexicon.

part for the whole. *See* synecdoche.

participle. *n.* A word that has characteristics of both a *verb and an *adjective—a "verbal adjective." As such, the Greek participle has gender, number and case (the adjectival side), as well as tense and voice (the verbal side).

particle. *n.* An *indeclinable word that conveys syntactical relationships or nuances of meaning, whose primary characteristic pertains to how it functions grammatically in a sentence rather than meaning inherent in the word itself. Particles are *function words. Some grammars treat conjunctions, negatives and other terms all under particles. A number of particles are small words (Lat. *particula*, "small part").

partitio. *n.* In rhetoric, a summary statement of the central thesis, what precisely is at issue. Also known as propositio. *See also* rhetorical criticism.

partitive genitive. *n.* A genitive that designates the whole of something, of which the *head noun is a part. Also referred to as wholative or genitive of the divided whole. See Luke 19:8; James 1:18; Revelation 11:13.

parts of speech. *n.* Classes of words grouped according to *grammatical function (e.g., noun, pronoun, verb, adverb, adjective, preposition, conjunction, etc.). In linguistics, sometimes called syntactic categories.

passive. *adj.* or *n.* The *voice that conveys that the *subject is being affected by or is the receiver of the verbal action.

passivum divinum. See divine passive.

past perfect. *See* pluperfect.

Pastoral Epistles. *n.* The New Testament letters of 1 and 2 Timothy and Titus, so named because of the ecclesiological matters and the pastoral concern expressed throughout.

pathos. *n.* In rhetoric, with regard to theories of argument and persuasion, knowledge of the audience and how they might be motivated. *See also* ethos and logos.

patois. *n.* A provincial or rural *dialect; or pejoratively, a "substandard" speech form (Fr. "dialect").

patristic citation/evidence. *n.* A biblical quotation or *allusion that appears in a writing by an early church father. Patristic evidence is helpful in *textual criticism as it gives us additional access to textual *readings extant in the early centuries of the church.

patronymic. *adj.* Of personal names, derived from the name of one's father or ancestor, especially by the addition of an *affix. —*n.* A patronymic name.

pattern word. *n.* A word that *declines according to a regular pattern and is therefore suitable for memorization.

Pauline. *adj.* Of or relating to Paul or the writings attributed to Paul.

Pauline corpus. *n.* All of the New Testament letters that claim to be written by Paul, including the *deutero-Pauline and *Pastoral Epistles.

Pauline privilege. *n.* Designation for Paul's allowance in 1 Corinthians 7:15 of divorce and possibly remarriage when an unbelieving spouse "departs," in which case the believer is "not bound."

Paulinism. *n.* An expression that is characteristically *Pauline.

pendent accusative. *n.* An accusative case substantive that is grammatically independent. This category can be subsumed by the *accusative of respect. See Matthew 21:42; Galatians 5:17.

pendent nominative. *n.* A grammatically independent nominative functioning as the subject of a sentence. See Luke 12:10; Acts 7:40; Revelation 3:12.

penult. *n.* The next-to-last syllable. Also called penultima.

penultimate. *adj.* or *n.* Of syllables, occurring next to last. Also penultima.

perfect. *adj.* or *n.* The *tense that normally denotes verbal action that has been completed in the past but which has present results.

perfect of completed action. *See* consummative perfect.

perfect of existing state. *See* consummative perfect.

perfective. *adj.* Of verbal action, portrayed as whole or complete.

perfective aorist. *See* consummative aorist.

performative language. *n.* Language that comprises a *speech act; it is causative. The language itself performs an action. See Luke 15:31; 22:29; 1 Corinthians 7:25. *See also* speech-act theory.

pericope. *n.* A paragraph or otherwise discrete section of writing, frequently the focus of *exegesis. The term is often restricted to the literary units in the Gospels. *pl.* pericopae or pericopes.

pericope adulterae. *n.* John 7:53—8:11, absent from a great number of early and diverse *witnesses. Also called the *pericope de adultera.*

period. *n.* A *sentence composed of several carefully balanced *clauses: a *main clause and a cluster of *dependent clauses. It is a "full" sentence, one that is rounded out (περί, "round" + ὁδός, "way").

periodic. *adj.* Of sentence structure or style, characterized by an intricate and carefully crafted relationship among its *clauses. *See* period.

peripeteia. *n.* In a narrative, a sudden or unexpected turn of events. See Mark 8:27-33; Luke 12:13-21. Also peripetia, peripety.

periphrasis. *n.* An indirect way of saying something (περίφρασις, "roundabout speech"). Same as *circumlocution. See 2 Corinthians 11:21—12:1; Colossians 2:1, 23.

periphrastic. *adj.* Roundabout; indirect. Or more technically it refers to a *construction in which a *participle occurs with a form of εἰμί.

periphrastic tense. *n.* The use of certain tenses (all but the aorist) together with εἰμί as an *auxiliary verb. See Luke 4:20; 12:6; 19:17; Ephesians 2:8.

perispomenon. *n.* A word having a *circumflex accent on the ultima (last *syllable) or penult (next-to-last syllable).

peristasis catalog. *See* hardship list.

permission imperative. Same as permissive imperative.

permissive imperative. *n.* The use of a third-person imperative mood verb to denote permission, toleration or allowance of the verbal action (usually translated "let him" or "let them").

permissive middle. *n.* The use of the middle voice to indicate that the subject allows something to be done to or for itself.

peroratio. *n.* In rhetoric, the conclusion of an argument, designed to reiterate the basic points and move an audience to take action. *See also* rhetorical criticism.

persistent accent. *n.* The tendency of the accent to remain on the same syllable of a word throughout its *declension.

person. *n.* The feature of verbs and pronouns that distinguishes speakers (first person), addressees (second person) and persons or things spoken of (third person). Person shows *grammatical roles (Lat. *persona*, "mask"). In Greek, person is marked in the verb itself by *personal endings; normally in English only the third person has a distinct *form (e.g., "I love," "you love," "he loves").

personal agency. *See* agency.

personal ending. *n.* A *suffix that indicates a verb's *person and *number. Personal endings are obviously used only with words that have person, namely, finite verbs. Case endings, on the other hand, are used with nouns, pronouns, adjectives and participles to indicate their case. Also called pronominal suffixes.

personal pronoun. *n.* A pronoun that takes the place of a noun that refers to a person.

personification. *n.* A *figure of speech in which human attributes are ascribed to objects, animals, abstract ideas or other nonpersonal things.

pesher. *n.* A type of Jewish interpretation of Scripture that emphasized present-day fulfillment (Heb. "interpretation"). Some of the *Dead Sea Scrolls are called pesherim.

Peshitta. *n.* The standard *version of the Syriac Bible (as the *Vulgate was in Latin), which was produced in the early part of the fifth century and contained only twenty-two books in the New Testament.

Petrusbriefe. Germ. "Peter's letters."

phenomenological criticism. *n.* Study of texts that begins with optimism regarding the fruitfulness of interpretation and an attempt to be theory-neutral and without presuppositions, which leads to simple reading of texts and an avoidance of abstractions.

Philo. *prop. n.* A first-century Jewish philosopher who lived and wrote in Alexandria, Egypt. —*n.* Shorthand for the writings of Philo.

philology. *n.* The study of the relationship of languages and the evolution of language over time. Sometimes called comparative philology or *linguistics or historical linguistics.

phone. *n.* The smallest perceptible discrete segment of sound in a stream of speech.

phoneme. *n.* A minimal unit in the sound system of a language. Phonemes are meaningful and distinctive in the sense that they contrast or distinguish words.

phonemic principle. *n.* The principle that (ideally) underlies alphabetic writing systems in which one symbol typically represents one *phoneme.

phonemics. *n.* The discipline concerned with language in terms of speech sounds (*phonemes) and the way they carry meaning.

phonetics. *n.* The discipline concerned with speech sounds in language, including how they are produced (articulatory phonetics), how they are perceived (auditory or perceptual phonetics) and the physical aspects of speech sounds (acoustic phonetics).

phonological processes. *n.* Systematic changes in language involving whole classes of sounds or sequences of sounds. These are driven by so-called phonological rules; they account for the sound patterns and constraints in a language. This behavior is sometimes termed phonotactics.

phonological rules. *See* phonological processes.

phonology. *n.* The discipline concerned with systems of speech sounds, how languages use the *distinctive features of sounds and follow predictable patterns in forming words.

phonotactics. *See* phonological processes.

phrase. *n.* A group of words within a *sentence or *clause that usually lacks the subject-predicate or subject-verb-object structure typical of clauses and sentences. Grammars will speak of noun, verb, adverbial, adjectival and prepositional phrases.

pidgin. *n.* A simple language that develops out of necessity so that communication can occur among speakers who do not know each other's language, and which is the native language of no one.

place name. *n.* A substantive that refers to a geographical location. Place names are regularly indeclinable.

play on words. *n.* A *pun. *See* paronomasia.

plenary genitive. *n.* A genitive substantive that is both *subjective and *objective. See Romans 5:5; 2 Corinthians 5:14.

pleonasm. *n.* The use of superfluous words or phrases (πλεονασμός, "having more than necessary"). *See also* circumlocution, otiose and tautology.

pleonastic participle. *See* redundant participle.

plosive. *n.* A speech sound made by complete closure in the mouth, followed by release of the blocked air. In Greek, this includes voiced (β, δ and γ) and voiceless (π, τ and κ) sounds. Sometimes used synonymously with *stop.

pluperfect. *adj.* or *n.* The *tense normally denoting an action that was completed in the past and whose results were also felt in the past (before the time of the speaker/writer). Also called the past perfect.

plural. *adj.* or *n.* Referring to more than one person or thing.

pluralize. *v.* To express in plural form.

polyglot. *n.* A book that displays the biblical text in three or more languages side by side for comparison. *See also* diglot.

polymorphemic. *adj.* Of words, consisting of more than one *morpheme.

polyptoton. *n.* In rhetoric, repetition of the same noun or pronoun in different cases at the start of two or more successive clauses. See Galatians 1:1.

polysemy. *n.* Diversity of meaning. E.g., ἀρχή can mean "beginning" or "ruler."

polysyllabic. *adj.* Having three or more syllables.

polysyndeton. *n.* The superfluous repetition of a *conjunction. It is the opposite of *asyndeton, the absence of a conjunction. See Romans 8:38-39; 9:4.

polyvalence. *n.* Multiplicity of meaning or significance in a text. *See also* poststructuralism and reader-response criticism.

position. *n.* The occurrence of language elements placed in a particular order (i.e., word order).

positive (degree). *adj.* Of adjectives and adverbs, denoting simple *attribution, as opposed to the *comparative or *superlative. The adjective *big* is a positive adjective, compared to *bigger* (comparative) and *biggest* (superlative).

positive for comparative. *n.* The use of a *positive adjective with a *comparative sense. See Matthew 18:8; 1 Corinthians 10:33.

positive for superlative. *n.* The use of a *positive adjective with a *superlative sense. See Matthew 22:38; Luke 9:48.

positive position. *See* primary position.

possessive. *adj.* Pertaining to ownership or possession. —*n.* A possessive pronoun.

possessive genitive. *n.* The use of a genitive substantive to denote ownership; the genitive is in some sense the possessor. See Matthew 26:51; James 3:3.

postpositive. *adj.* Not occurring first in a clause. —*n.* A word that cannot occur first. Postpositives include γάρ, δέ and οὖν.

poststructural criticism. *See* poststructuralism.

poststructuralism. *n.* In the study of texts, an approach that, unlike *structuralism, sees language as a system whose value and meaning are indeterminate, shifting according to nonlinguistic factors.

potential optative. *n.* The use of the optative in *fourth class conditions. See Acts 8:31; 17:18.

pragmatics. *n.* The branch of *linguistics concerned with "speaker meaning"—how meaning is conveyed. This involves, among other things, the relationship between speech and the shared presuppositions among those who communicate.

predicate. *n.* The part of a clause consisting of a verb and often other components that *complement the *subject, expressing (predicating) something about it; the element or construction around which the sentence is organized. Also called a verb *phrase and a *comment. The term may also be used as shorthand for the *predicate nominative.

predicate accusative. *n.* An accusative substantive or adjective that together with a verbal form functions as the predicate of a clause, asserting something about another accusative substantive. See 1 Timothy 1:12-13; James 1:8.

predicate adjective. *n.* An adjective that occurs with an *equative verb and describes the *subject.

predicate nominative. *n.* A substantive in the nominative case that is joined to a subject by an *equative verb (εἰμί or γίνομαι) and refers to the same person or thing as the subject. See John 1:1; 4:24.

predicate position. *n.* A construction that appears with an *equative verb and consists of an articular noun and an adjective or participle that is not immediately preceded by the article. Thus it predicates something about the noun. *See also* first-predicate position and second-predicate position.

predictive future. *n.* A future-tense verb denoting action that will take place in the future. See John 14:26; 1 Corinthians 15:51, 52.

preface. *n.* A preliminary section of a literary work.

preferred reading. *n.* In textual criticism, a particular rendering of a passage found in one or more witnesses that is judged to be superior to the others.

prefix. *n.* A *morpheme affixed to the front of a word, including inflectional changes.

preformative. *adj.* Prefixed. —*n.* A *prefix.

pregnant construction. *n.* An elliptical construction (*see* ellipsis) that implies more than what is actually written. Also referred to as *constructio praegnans*. See Luke 6:8.

preposition. *n.* An *indeclinable word that governs a *prepositional phrase, indicating the relationship between a *substantive and another word—a verb, adjective or another substantive.

prepositional. *adj.* Consisting of, used as or somehow related to a *preposition.

prepositional phrase. *n.* A phrase consisting of a *preposition and a substantive that has *adjectival or *adverbial force.

prepositional prefix. *n.* A prefixed *preposition.

prescript. *n.* The formal start of a letter or *epistle, which in New Testament times normally included the name of the author/sender, the addressee, a greeting and a blessing or prayer.

prescriptive grammar. *n.* Language study concerned with providing rules for proper usage. Language study can be prescriptive, describing how a language ought to be used, or it can be descriptive, simply observing how people converse. For example, one can say that it is improper to split infinitives (based on Latin!), but native English speakers will continue to unwittingly do it. *See also* descriptive grammar.

present. *adj.* or *n.* The *tense that normally expresses *progressive action occurring in the present.

preterit. *n.* In English grammar, the simple past tense (e.g., *ran*). Also preterite.

pretonic. *adj.* Of syllables, immediately preceding the *tonic syllable, which has the prominent *accent.

primary agency. *See* agency.

primary endings. *n.* The group of *personal endings used on present-, future- and perfect-tense verb forms. *See also* secondary endings.

primary position. *adj.* or *n.* Occurring at the front of a clause. Also called positive position.

primary tenses. *n.* The present, future and perfect tenses in the indicative, all following the same pattern in their *personal endings.

primary version. *n.* A *translation produced directly from the original language, as opposed to a *secondary version, produced from a primary version.

primitive Mark. *See* Urmarkus.

principal clause. *See* main clause.

principal part. *n.* The basic form of a verb as it occurs in a particular tense. Also called the tense stem. Often grammars will include a lexicon or a verb list that displays the principal parts of verbs. The six principal parts of a verb are often presented in this order: present active, future active, aorist active, perfect active, perfect middle/passive and aorist passive.

Prison Epistles. *pl. n.* The letters of Paul, excluding the Pastorals, that he is thought to have written while incarcerated: Ephesians, Philippians, Colossians and Philemon.

privative. *n.* An element added to a word that changes it from a positive to a *negative. *See also* alpha privative.

probatio. *n.* In rhetoric, the main body of an argument, in which the reasons for one's point of view are set forth. *See also* rhetorical criticism.

process present. *See* customary present.

proclitic. *n.* A word having no *accent of its own but which depends (προκλίνω, "lean forward") on the following word for accent (e.g., εἰ, ὁ, οὐ, ὡς). *See also* enclitic.

proclivi scriptioni praestat ardua. Lat. "the harder reading is more likely." *See* more difficult reading.

prodiorthosis. *n.* In rhetoric, a remark prefaced to a difficult or unpalatable argument. Such a statement, if it *follows* the argument, is called *epidiorthosis. See 2 Corinthians 11:1, 16, 21, 23.

proem. *n.* A preface or preamble.

progressive action. *n.* Verbal action that denotes continuity or that which is ongoing. Also called continuous or descriptive action.

progressive assimilation. *n.* A consonant sound becoming more like the preceding consonant. *See also* assimilation and regressive assimilation.

progressive future. *n.* A future-tense verb denoting ongoing future action. See Romans 6:2; Philippians 1:6, 18.

progressive imperfect. *n.* A present-tense verb that is used of ongoing (progressive) action occurring in the past. Also known as the *descriptive imperfect. See Mark 12:41; John 11:36.

progressive present. *n.* A present-tense verb that denotes ongoing action in the present. Also known as the descriptive present. See Matthew 25:8; Galatians 1:6.

progressive stem. *n.* The stem of a verb in its lexical form, which is used to form the *present and *imperfect.

prohibition imperative. *n.* The use of μή plus an imperative mood verb to state a negative command.

prohibitive subjunctive. *n.* A second-person aorist subjunctive verb used to express a prohibition, as in "Do not worry about tomorrow."

Also termed the prohibition or prohibitory subjunctive. See Matthew 6:13, 34; Hebrews 3:8.

prolegomena. *pl. n.* Preliminary matters (*sg.* prolegomenon). The term often refers to books or sections of books that deal with prefatory issues.

prolepsis. *n.* The transfer of a word from a *dependent clause to the *main clause. See Mark 1:24; Revelation 3:9. In rhetoric, it refers to treating a future event as if it already happened or to a device in which one brings up an objection to one's own argument before an opponent can. *See also* antiptosis.

proleptic. *adj.* Anticipatory; future-referring.

proleptic accusative. *n.* A noun or pronoun in the accusative, not strictly because of function, but because it has been transferred from one clause (in which it would have been nominative) to another. This is an example of *antiptosis. See Mark 1:24.

proleptic aorist. *n.* An aorist tense verb that describes a future event as if it were already completed. Also called futuristic aorist. See John 13:31; 15:6; 17:18; Romans 8:30.

prologue. *n.* A precursory section of a literary work, often introducing *motifs and salient features.

pronominal. *adj.* Derived from a pronoun. E.g., *his* in the sentence "Dennis is his son," is a pronominal adjective. —*n.* A pronoun.

pronominal suffix. *n.* A verbal ending that conveys the subject's person and number. Also called personal ending.

pronoun. *n.* A word that stands in the place of a noun. In Greek, there are *demonstrative, *indefinite, *interrogative, *personal, *possessive, *reciprocal, *reflexive and *relative pronouns.

pronouncement story. *n.* In *form criticism, a brief narrative whose main point is a pronouncement by Jesus. A pronouncement story can be an expanded version of a *chreia. Similar to *paradigms and *apothegms.

prooemium. *n.* A brief introductory part of an address or literary work designed to win over an audience. *See also* exordium, proem.

prooftext. *n.* An Old Testament quotation brought forward to prove a point only, often with little explanation and without emphasis on the original historical setting, context or meaning. —*v.* To cite a prooftext.

proparaskeue. *n.* In rhetoric, a statement prefaced to an argument that in some sense prepares the audience. See Philippians 1:12.

proparoxytone. *n.* A word having an *acute accent on the antepenult, the third syllable from the last. *See also* barytone, oxytone and paroxytone.

proper diphthong. *n.* A genuine *diphthong, as opposed to an *improper diphthong (i.e., a vowel with an *iota subscript).

proper noun. *n.* A noun that refers to a particular object (e.g., *Thomas*, *Sunday)*, usually a person, thing or temporal name. A *common noun, on the other hand, refers to one or all of the members of a class generally.

proper preposition. *n.* A preposition that functions solely as a preposition and can be prefixed to a verb. *See also* improper preposition.

prophetia post eventum. Lat. "prophecy after the fact." *See vaticinium ex eventu.*

propositio. *See* partitio.

prosapodosis. *n.* In rhetoric, the mention of two or more words or subjects, with a return to them again, where they are repeated, for explanation or clarification (προσαπόδοσις, "returning"). See John 16:8-11; 1 Corinthians 14:1-3.

prose. *n.* Writing that reproduces ordinary spoken language, as opposed to verse.

prosopopoeia. *n.* The attribution of speech or personality to nonhumans. See 1 Corinthians 12:12-26.

prospective. *adj.* Pointing forward. See Philemon 15.

prostaxis. *See* parataxis.

protasis. *n.* In a *conditional sentence, the clause that presents a condition or a hypothesis (the "if" clause); the counterpart of the *apodosis (the "then" clause).

prothesis. *n.* The addition of a *short vowel (the prothetic vowel) in word-initial position.

prothetic vowel. *See* prothesis.

proto-Luke. *n.* A hypothetical document or draft believed by some to stand behind the Gospel of Luke.

proto-Mark. *n.* A hypothetical document or draft believed by some to stand behind the Gospel of Mark.

proto-Theodotion recension. *See* Kaige recension.

provenance. *n.* Place of origin (Lat. *provenire*, "to come forth"). Determining the provenance of the New Testament writings is done by evaluating internal evidence and external evidence (early church writings and datable historical events).

proverbial. *See* gnomic.

pseudepigraphic. *adj.* Written under a false name. Also pseudonymous. *See also* Old Testament Pseudepigrapha and New Testament Pseudepigrapha.

pseudo-Pauline. *See* deutero-Pauline epistles.

pseudonym. *n.* A fictitious name assumed for authoring a literary work; a pen name.

pseudonymity. *n.* The practice of authoring a literary work under a fictitious name. A large number of Jewish, Christian and pagan writings from antiquity were pseudonymous.

psilosis. *n.* The tendency toward *deaspiration; that is, a decrease in the use of the "h" sound.

psycholinguistics. *n.* Linguistic study concerned specifically with the relationship of the mind and language, communication and the underlying psychological processes. More specifically, this can include study of linguistic performance, language acquisition and speech production and comprehension.

pun. *n.* A play on words usually involving different senses of the same word or a *homophone. *See also* paronomasia.

punctiliar. *adj.* Denoting action that occurs instantaneously or at a point in time, as opposed to action that is progressive, ongoing; or action that is conceived of as a whole or as a point.

punctiliar aorist. *See* constative aorist.

punctiliar present. *See* instantaneous present.

pure. *adj.* complete; unmixed; containing nothing extraneous. The term is used in various ways: of the pronunciation of vowel sounds that are not *diphthongs or *glides; of *conjugations in which a particular vowel appears consistently; and of tense usage when a particular sample conveys the basic sense of that tense.

pure perfect. *See* consummative perfect.

purpose. *adj.* Of infinitives, participles, subjunctives, whole clauses and other elements, denoting purpose.

pusma. *n.* In rhetoric, a question that requires an answer other than yes or no. See Romans 3:1.

Q

Q. *n.* A hypothetical sayings source, discussed in the search for a solution to the *synoptic problem, thought by many to have been used by Matthew and Luke (Germ. *Quelle,* "source"). This involves material common to Matthew and Luke and not found in Mark; Q being the putative source of that sayings material. A Q hypothesis helps to explain strong verbal agreement between these two Gospels. Likewise it can refer to material that is common to Matthew and Luke without comment on the viability of a Q hypothesis. *See also* Two-Source and Four-Source hypotheses.

qal wahomer. n. One of the rules or techniques of midrashic interpretation (*see* midrash) that states that what applies in a less-important case applies all the more in a more-important case (Heb. "light and heavy"). *See also a fortiori.*

qualitative. *adj.* Pertaining to a quality or the nature of something.

qualitative vowel gradation. *n. See* ablaut.

quarto. *n.* A sheet folded twice and cut to make a total of four leaves or eight pages; or a book made of such pages. E.g., Codex Vaticanus is a quarto volume. *See also* folio and octavo. Also quaternion.

quaternion. *See* quarto.

Quelle. Germ. "source." *See* Q.

Quellenkritik. Germ. "source criticism." *See* literary criticism.

question. *n.* A language form that inquires, calling for a reply (unless it is a *rhetorical question).

quire. *n.* A book made from several sheets that are compiled, folded and stitched.

Qumran. *See* Dead Sea Scrolls

R

rational criticism. *See* rigorous eclecticism.

reader-response criticism. *n.* The discipline concerned with biblical interpretation, with special attention to how a reader responds to a text: the way in which a text directs readers and the way fresh meaning can be created when a reader encounters a text.

reading. *n.* In textual criticism, any divergence in a segment of text in one *manuscript as compared with the same segment of text in any other manuscript. *See also* variant.

reasoned eclecticism. *n.* An approach to textual criticism that does not look to a single text or *text-type as the standard, but rather deals with variants on a case-by-case basis, allowing one principle to govern all other considerations: the *variant that best accounts for the others is most likely to be the original. Also referred to as genuine or moderate eclecticism, the *eclectic method or the local-genealogical method.

Received Text. *n. See* Textus Receptus.

recension. *n.* In textual criticism, a revision of an earlier text or document. More broadly, the term can refer to any *manuscript, assuming that it is an inexact copy.

receptor language. *See* target language.

recessive accent. *n.* The tendency of the accent to move away from the last syllable of a word.

reciprocal middle. *n.* The use of a third-person, middle-voice verb to indicate verbal action that is done in an interactive (reciprocal) way. There is action among the constituents of the plural subject, usually made explicit by the use of ἀλλήλων.

reciprocal pronoun. *n.* The use of ἀλλήλων, which denotes reciprocal action. See 1 Thessalonians 5:11, 15; 1 Peter 5:5, 14.

recitative ὅτι. *n.* The use of the conjunction ὅτι to introduce a *direct quotation. In such a case it is left untranslated. Also referred to as *recitativum*. See Colossians 2:9.

recitativum. See recitative ὅτι.

recto. *n.* The right-hand side of an open *codex, as opposed to *verso. Also, the front of a papyrus leaf (Lat. "right").

redaction. *n.* The process or result of modifying or editing a text.

redaction criticism. *n.* The discipline that seeks to recognize the alterations made by the *Evangelists to the written sources they possessed as well as the theological perspective that was driving their composition. In addition, a redaction critic may propose a setting for the emergence of the Evangelist's own views. The term translates the German *Redaktionsgeschichte.* Sometimes referred to as composition criticism (Germ. *Kompositionsgeschichte*), a term that emphasizes the Evangelist as author and not mere redactor.

Redaktionsgeschichte. See redaction criticism.

redundant middle. *n.* The use of the middle voice along with a *reflexive pronoun. See 2 Timothy 2:13; James 1:22.

redundant participle. *n.* A participle that idiomatically qualifies or complements a finite verb, usually one of saying, thinking, seeming, etc. Also called the appositional, idiomatic or pleonastic participle.

reduplication. *n.* Duplication of the initial letter or sound of a verb to mark it as perfect or pluperfect. When the word begins with a vowel or diphthong, *lengthening occurs instead.

reference. *n.* In *semantics, that which a word or expression stands for. This can involve a word's *denotation, or it can point to the actual thing in the world that is signified by a word or expression.

referent. *n.* That which is being referred to.

referential meaning. *See* denotation.

reflexive. *adj.* Of prepositions, verbs and other constructions, denoting verbal ideas in which the subject and object refer to the same person or thing; the subject acts on itself. Or more narrowly, of verb forms in which the subject is affected by its own action.

reflexive active. *n.* The use of the active voice along with a *reflexive pronoun to indicate that the subject acts upon itself. It is functionally equivalent to the basic sense of the *middle voice, but more explicit.

reflexive middle. *See* direct middle.

reflexive pronoun. *n.* A pronoun that conveys a *reflexive sense; the subject of the main verb is its antecedent. See Philippians 2:7; 1 John 1:8.

regimen. *n.* The relationship of a governing *noun (i.e., *head noun) and its genitive; they are said to be "in regimen" (Lat. "rule, government").

regional original. *See* local text.

register. *n.* A variety of language reserved for use in certain social settings. The term can also refer to phonetic voice quality.

regressive assimilation. *n.* A consonant sound becoming more like a following consonant (e.g., ἐν + μένω becomes ἐμμένω). *See also* assimilation and progressive assimilation.

regular. *adj.* Normal, according to expectation. Often certain forms, inflections or paradigms will be described as regular since they conform to the normal pattern.

relational genitive. *n.* A genitive that identifies a personal relationship such as familial relationship. Also called *genitive of relationship.

relative. *adj.* Referring back to or qualifying an *antecedent. —*n.* A relative pronoun, adjective, adverb or clause.

relative clause. *n.* A *dependent clause introduced by a *relative pronoun. Relative clauses can function in a variety of ways, including like nouns or adjectives.

relative pronoun. *n.* A pronoun that introduces a *relative clause. Relative pronouns have gender, case and number. The gender and number of the relative pronoun will conform to its *antecedent. Its case is determined by its function in its own clause.

relative time. *n.* The indication of *time in a verbal element (usually a participle) that is relative to another component in the sentence, as opposed to *absolute time, which is not.

religio-historical criticism. *n.* The discipline concerned with the comparative study of religions. Also referred to as comparative religion or *Religionsgeschichte*.

Religionsgeschichte. Germ. "History of religion." *See* religio-historical criticism.

Religionsgeschichtliche Schule. Germ. "History of religions school." *See* religio-historical criticism.

reported speech. *See* indirect discourse.

restrictive. *adj.* Of modifying words and phrases, essential to the identity of the *head noun.

result clause. *See* consecutive clause.

result participle. *n.* An adverbial participle that denotes result. Also called the consecutive participle. The same terminology is used of the infinitive and the subjunctive.

resultative aorist. *See* consummative aorist.

resultative perfect. *See* consummative perfect.

resumptive. *adj.* Recapitulating or tending to take up again after a break or interruption.

retained object. *n.* The *object that, in an *active object-complement construction, is retained when it is converted to a *passive.

retrospective. *adj.* Pointing back.

reverse genitive. *See* attributed genitive.

rhetoric. *n.* The study and practice of the craft of effective communication, especially argumentation and the art of persuasion. *See also* rhetorical criticism.

rhetorical analysis. *See* rhetorical criticism.

rhetorical criticism. *n.* The discipline concerned with the interpretation of the biblical text from the perspective of classical *rhetoric, using the technical terms related to methods of argumentation, *figures of speech and *tropes. Frequently six Latin terms denoting the parts of a typical rhetorical composition or speech are listed: *exordium, *narratio, *partitio (or propositio), *probatio, *exhortatio and *peroratio. The term can also be used more broadly of any interpretive approach that emphasizes rhetorical and literary theory, including the interpretation of literary units by recognizing characteristics of *genre, structural patterns, rhetorical devices and stylistic features.

rhetorical device. *See* literary device.

rhetorical question. *n.* A statement that resembles a question but does not require a response.

rigorous eclecticism. *n.* An approach to *textual criticism that relies almost exclusively on *internal evidence: intrinsic and *transcriptional probabilities. Also referred to as consistent, rational or thoroughgoing eclecticism.

root. *n.* The most basic form of a word. Grammars use terms such as *root* and *stem* to convey the notion of basic forms undergoing changes in different *declensions and *inflections.

root fallacy. *See* etymological fallacy.

root word. *See* root.

rough breathing. *n.* The *diacritical mark (ἁ) that stands above word-initial vowels and signifies an "h" sound in the pronunciation of the vowel. Also called *spiritus asper*. Or the "h" sound indicated by that diacritic.

rounded vowel. *n.* A vowel sound produced with rounding of the lips.

running hand. *See* cursive.

S

Sachhälfte. Germ. "reality half." —*n.* The part of a *parable that constitutes the meaningful content or "reality," as opposed to the imagery or mental picture that is depicted *(*Bildhälfte).*

sacred history. *See* salvation-history.

salvation-history. *n.* A theological perspective of history and the unfolding biblical narrative with emphasis on the divine plan, God's redemptive purposes and the theme of promise and fulfillment. Also called sacred history or *Heilsgeschichte*.

Sammelgattungen. Germ. "collected forms."

sayings source. *n.* A hypothetical source document behind Matthew and Luke, suggested to explain the fact that they both seem to have relied on a source for the "sayings" of Jesus. Usually referred to as *Q.

schema atticum. n. The *grammatical rule of classical Greek writers that a neuter plural subject takes a singular verb. The New Testament writers usually followed the rule with a nonpersonal or abstract noun, but not with personal nouns.

schema etymologicum. See cognate accusative.

scholia. *pl. n.* Interpretive notes usually written in the margin of a *manuscript. Frequent scholia on a single text constitute a *commentary. *sg.* scholion.

scribal gloss. *See* gloss.

scribal tendencies. *See* transcriptional probability.

scribe. *n.* In textual criticism, one who serves as a writer or *copyist. Also copyist.

scriptio continua. Lat. "continuous script." *See* cursive.

scriptoria. Plural of *scriptorium.

scriptorium. *n.* A room in a monastery where the *copyists worked.

second aorist. *n.* A verb that in the aorist tense behaves according to an observable pattern in its *inflections; it uses a different form of the verbal stem than the present (for this reason it is called *irregular), and it does not have an "infixed" sigma (as *first aorists do). Whether a verb is a first aorist or a second aorist has no bearing whatsoever on its meaning; rather, aorist verbs happen to decline according to two clearly identifiable patterns, and they are classified this way to aid the student.

second attributive position. *n.* The position of an adjective when it appears in the sequence article-noun-article-adjective.

second class condition. *n.* A *conditional sentence in which the premise of the *protasis (the "if" clause) is assumed to be false or is presented as false for the sake of argument. This is conveyed using εἰ plus a verb in the indicative mood in the protasis and usually ἄν plus the indicative in the *apodosis (the "then" clause). Sometimes called the unreal condition or the contrary-to-fact condition.

second declension. *n.* The inflectional pattern (*see* inflection) for words whose *stems end in omicron (comprised mostly of masculine words).

second predicate position. *n.* The position of an adjective when it appears in the sequence article-noun-adjective.

Second Temple period. *n.* The period from the rebuilding of the temple in Jerusalem (ca. 515 B.C.) until A.D. 70, when it was destroyed.

secondary agency. *See* agent.

secondary endings. *n.* The group of *personal endings used on aorist, imperfect and pluperfect tense verb forms. *See also* primary endings.

secondary tense. *n.* A tense that takes the *augment; i.e., the aorist, imperfect and pluperfect tenses.

secondary version. *n.* A *translation produced not from the original language, but from a *primary version (i.e., a translation).

segment. *n.* In linguistics, any discrete unit in a language that can be identified in speech.

segmental contrasts. *See* distinctive feature.

semantic domain. *n.* The broad category of meaning in which a word is to be understood, especially as it relates to other similar words. Semantic domain theory organizes a language's vocabulary into groups of words related in meaning (according to *sense relations), so that words can interrelate and define each other.

semantic field. *See* semantic domain.

semantics. *n.* The study of meaning in language.

semasiology. *See* semantics.

semiology. *See* semiotics.

semiotics. *n.* The study of communication as a vast system of signs (σημειότικος, "observant of signs"). Synonymous with semiology.

Semitic Greek. *See* Septuagint Greek.

Semitism. *n.* Any characteristic of the Semitic languages—particularly Hebrew and *Aramaic—that resonates in the Greek style of the New Testament and the *Septuagint. Or the term can refer more broadly to *literary forms and distinctively Jewish content. Semitisms can be explained because of the integration of cultures, including bilingualism, as well as the influence the Septuagint held during the first century. Semitisms is the broader descriptive term for *Hebraisms and *Aramaisms more specifically. Also Semiticism.

semivowel. *n.* A speech sound that functions as a consonant, but lacking some of the typical characteristics of consonants, it has the phonetic quality of a vowel.

sense. *n.* In *semantics, the meaning attached to words, especially as it comes to the surface in relationship to other words.

sense gender. *See* natural gender.

sense relations. *n.* The system of linguistic relationships, such as synonymy (*see* synonym) and antonymy (*see* antonym), that exist between words. *See also* semantic domain.

sensus plenior. *n.* The fuller sense of a biblical passage, which was not intended or understood by the original author (Lat. "fuller sense"). E.g., frequently when a New Testament author quotes a passage from the Old Testament, the question of *sensus plenior*—meaning that goes beyond the original sense—rises to the surface.

sentence. *n.* A grammatical construction made up of a number of elements—usually a *subject and a *predicate—so that it is thought of as complete and independent.

sentence structure. *n.* The makeup of a sentence; how its different parts are arranged.

Septuagint. *n.* The Greek translation of the Old Testament produced around 200 B.C. to accommodate Hellenization. The Septuagint rapidly became *the* Bible of synagogue worship and Jewish instruction, and in the New Testament is cited more frequently than the original Hebrew. Tradition said that there were seventy translators (Lat. *septuaginta*, "seventy"; abbreviated LXX). In their translating they were, quite naturally, heavily influenced by the Old Testament; an echo of Septuagintal idiosyncrasies is also found in certain New Testament writers. *See also* Aramaism, Semitism.

Septuagint Greek. *n.* A style of Greek found in the *Septuagint, peculiar because of the way it imitates the original Hebrew and *Aramaic of the Old Testament. It is observed that Luke, particularly in his birth narratives (chaps. 1-2), uses a Septuagintal style (sometimes referred to as "Septuagintalisms") much like someone today might use the archaic language of the King James Version, achieving an effect of language that sounds lofty and "religious." Sometimes called Semitic Greek. *See also* Aramaism, Semitism.

Septuagintism. *n.* A word or phrase that is derived from or reminiscent of the *Septuagint. *See* Septuagint Greek.

sermocinatio. *n.* In rhetoric, the fabrication of statements, conversations, soliloquies or thoughts. See 1 Corinthians 1:12.

setting in life. *See* Sitz im Leben.

Sharp's rule. *See* Granville Sharp rule.

short vowel. *n.* A vowel sound whose duration when uttered was originally shorter relative to other vowels, but now is differentiated solely on the basis of its quality (the sound produced as a result of the *manner of articulation).

shorter reading. *n.* A variation of a text that contains fewer words, which may indicate that it is *original. Its probable originality is due to the fact that *scribes were more inclined to add than delete material. *See also lectio brevior potior.*

sibilant. *n.* A speech sound articulated with friction made by the tongue at the back of the roof of the mouth. Sibilants are a class of sounds that includes *alveolar and *palatal *fricatives and *affricates.

sigla. Plural of *siglum.

siglum. *n.* An abbreviation or symbol. *pl.* sigla.

significant. *adj.* or *n.* In linguistics, a feature of language that carries meaning or changes meaning by its presence or absence.

signs source. *n.* A hypothetical document that many scholars believe served as a source for John's Gospel, evidently narrating a number of Jesus' miracles.

simile. *n.* A comparison of two basically unlike things, frequently using the word *like* or *as* (Lat. *similis*, "alike"). See 1 Corinthians 3:10. *See also* metaphor.

similitude. *n.* An *allegory or *parable.

simple aorist. *See* constative aorist.

simple condition. *See* first class condition.

simple sentence. *n.* A main clause with no *dependent clauses.

simple stem. *n.* The stem of a verb used to form the future and the aorist tense.

simultaneous action. *adj.* Verbal action occurring at the same time as some other action.

Sinaiticus. *See* Codex Sinaiticus.

singular. *adj.* Referring to one person or thing.

singular reading. *n.* In textual criticism, a *variant reading that is supported by only one Greek manuscript.

Sitz im Leben. Germ. "setting in life." This refers to the origin of the New Testament writings: those sociological situations or church needs that gave rise to the distinctive character of a particular *form or *literary unit. *pl. Sitze im Leben.*

Sitz im Leben Jesu. Germ. "Setting in the life of Jesus."

Sitz im Leben Kirche. Germ. "Setting in the life of the church." *See Sitz im Leben.*

slot. *n.* In linguistics, a place in a grammatical construction into which a class of words can be inserted (*fillers).

smooth breathing. *n.* The *diacritical mark (ἀ) that stands above word-initial vowels and signifies ordinary pronunciation of the vowel sound. Also called *spiritus lenis.* Or the pronunciation of the vowel without the "h" sound as indicated by that diacritic.

social-scientific criticism. *n.* A method of interpreting a text by attempting to reconstruct the social situation of the community that lay behind it. Also referred to as the sociohistorical method.

sociative dative. *See* dative of association.

sociohistorical method. *See* social-scientific criticism.

sociolinguistics. *n.* Language study concerned specifically with the linguistic aspect of social behavior. This can entail such things as the place of language in achieving social identity, speakers' attitudes toward language and social levels of language.

sociological criticism. *n.* The discipline concerned with interpretation of the biblical text with special attention to the societal factors that helped shape the faith community and its writings.

sociorhetorical criticism. *n.* The discipline concerned with the interpretation of the biblical text with special sensitivity to the way in which an author uses *forms, traditions and rhetorical or *literary devices to connect with an audience and communicate.

solecism. *n.* A violation of standard *grammatical usage. See Colossians 3:14.

sonorant. *n.* A class of speech sounds that includes vowels, glides, liquids and nasals. Also referred to as nonobstruents.

sorites. *n.* A sequence of propositions in which one established *predicate becomes the *subject of the next proposition. *See also* climax.

source criticism. *n.* The discipline concerned with trying to identify the sources behind a literary unit or work. In Gospel studies, similar wording, content and order of material necessitate investigation of source-critical issues. See Luke 1:1-4.

source language. *n.* The language from which a *translation originates, as opposed to the *target or receptor language.

speech act. *n.* The nonlinguistic accomplishments of an utterance. *See* speech-act theory.

speech-act theory. *n.* Linguistic theory that focuses on the use of language to perform certain actions, such as blessing, naming, etc. *See also* performative language.

spirant. *See* fricative.

spiritus asper. Lat. "*rough breathing."

spiritus lenis. Lat. "soft breathing." *See* smooth breathing.

spurious diphthong. *n.* A *diphthong (specifically ει or ου) that arises from vowel *contraction or *compensatory lengthening.

spurious reading. *n.* In textual criticism, a particular rendering of a passage that is judged to be inauthentic.

staging. *n.* The prominence given to a particular *discourse element in relation to other elements (the ordering of material, repetition, etc.).

stanza. *n.* A group of lines of poetry, usually related by a pattern or a theme. It is the equivalent in poetry of the *paragraph. Also called a strophe.

static. *See* stative.

stative. *adj.* Of verbal action, denoting a state or condition. For example, a stative present is a present-tense verb that speaks of a condition or ongoing state of being; a stative active uses the active voice and describes a state, etc.

stem. *n.* The essential part of a word as it appears in a given tense; the basic *morpheme in each *principal part.

stem formative. *n.* A letter or group of letters that attach to the *root or *stem of a word so that a *suffix can then be added. The term *tense formative* is used specifically of formative elements added to produce the tense endings (usually a vowel). The term *stem formative* is broader, signifying any formative element.

stemma. *n.* A genealogy of *manuscripts that traces the *transmission of a text in its *recensions or the relationship of *text-types; a "family tree" of manuscript recensions.

stemma codicum. *n.* A diagram that displays the history of *transmission. Also called a genealogical chart.

stemmatic method. *See* genealogical method.

stichometric reckoning. *n.* The calculation of the length or accuracy of a manuscript by counting stichoi (lines of text; *see* stichos).

stichometry. *n.* A method of transcription that involves calculating and arranging text according to the number of lines. *See* stichos.

stichos. *n.* A line of text in a manuscript, often having a standard number of syllables by which a *copyist calculated his pay rate. *pl.* stichoi.

Stichwort. *n.* A "stitch word" or "catch word" that ties together concepts or themes in a text. In New Testament studies, for example, the use of *Stichwort* is frequently discussed as one of the organizational methods of the author of Hebrews. With reference to dictionaries, the term refers to the lexical entry under which the definition is given. *pl.* *Stichworte.*

stop. *n.* A speech sound in which the flow of air is completely stopped. Also called *plosives.

strong verb. *n.* A verb that conforms to the regular pattern. Also called a regular verb or a root verb.

strophe. *See* stanza.

structural analysis. *See* grammatical analysis.

structural criticism. *See* structuralism.

structural linguistics. *See* structuralism.

structuralism. *n.* Any study of language explicitly in terms of its structures and systems; likewise the study of language in terms of recognizable, culturally-conditioned systems and interrelated features that are meaning producing; or sometimes more broadly of the nonlinguistic structures of human self-expression (relationships, behaviors, institutions) and their inherent modes of thought. Also called stylistic criticism or structural *exegesis.

structure. *n.* *See* sentence structure.

structure marker. *n.* A conjunction, preposition or relative pronoun that clues in the reader or listener to the relationship of clauses and the structure of a *discourse.

style. *n.* Of literature, a general term for the way in which something is written. It pertains to a work's distinctive rhetorical features and *literary devices, vocabulary and the choice of words, the frequency or paucity of certain grammatical constructions, and the sense of the writer's influences, among other things.

stylistic criticism. *See* structural criticism.

stylistics. *n.* The study of human language in terms of definable tendencies and characteristics of a speaker/author.

stylus. *n.* A pointed writing instrument.

subgenre. *n.* A category of literary composition (*see* genre) that does not affect an entire work.

subject. *n.* The major component of a sentence; the performer of the action with *active verbs, the receiver of the action with *middle voice and *passive verbs; and that which is being described with *equative verbs. Also called the topic.

subject complement. *n.* Another term for a *predicate nominative or a *predicate adjective.

subject of the infinitive. *n.* An accusative noun or pronoun that indicates the subject of the action of the *infinitive.

subjective genitive. *n.* A genitive substantive that functions as the *subject (i.e., it performs the action) of the verbal action implied in the *head noun. See Romans 8:35; 1 Corinthians 16:17; 1 John 5:9.

subjunctive. *adj.* or *n.* The *mood that presents the verbal action as being possible or probable.

subordinate clause. *See* dependent clause.

subordinate conjunction. *n.* A conjunction that introduces a dependent (subordinate) clause.

subordination. *n.* The joining of unequal grammatical units, one being dependent on the other. *See also* hypotaxis.

subsequent action. *n.* Action that occurs after some other action.

subsingular reading. *n.* In textual criticism, a *variant reading that has only secondary support, namely, support in the inferior Greek manuscripts, versions or the fathers; or a reading that has agreement that is accidental, that is, between two manuscripts that are not otherwise closely related.

substantival. *adj.* Of the nature of a *substantive (functionally equivalent to a noun). For example, in the sentence "let the dead bury their dead," the *adjective *dead* is substantival.

substantive. *n.* A *noun or any word or group of words that functions like a noun, that is, that fills the "noun *slot." Pronouns, adjectives, infinitives, participles and even whole clauses can be substantival.

subtext. *n.* An implicit meaning or theme in a text. Or a text that is embedded in another text or that stands behind an *allusion.

suffix. *n.* A *morpheme affixed to the end of a word.

summary aorist. *See* constative aorist.

superlative. *adj.* Of adjectives and adverbs, denoting comparison that speaks of the highest degree. The adjective *biggest* is a superlative adjective, compared to *big* (*positive) and *bigger* (*comparative). Called the superlative degree.

superlative for comparative. *n.* The use of a *superlative adjective with a *comparative sense, as in the expression "May the best man win," meaning "May the *better* man between us win." See Matthew 21:28; 1 Timothy 2:13; Hebrews 8:7.

superlative for elative. *n.* The use of a *superlative adjective with an *elative sense, as in "You're the greatest," meaning "You're very great." See Mark 4:1; 1 Corinthians 4:3.

superordinate clause. *n.* The *main clause, as opposed to a *dependent clause.

supplementary participle. *See* complementary participle.

suppletion. *n.* The appearance of a word in a conjugational pattern (*see* conjugation) or paradigm with an anomalous *stem. Suppletion involves so-called *defective verbs.

supporting genre. *See* subgenre.

suprasegmental feature. *n.* A feature of spoken language that extends over more than one sound *segment in an utterance, such as stress or pitch.

suspended case. *See casus pendens.*

suspension. *n.* In textual criticism, a type of abbreviation used by *scribes in which only the first part of a word is written and the remaining letters are superscripted, replaced by a horizontal line or some other mark, or dropped altogether. *See also nomina sacra.*

syllabic augment. *n.* The *augmentation of a *tense stem that results in the addition of a syllable.

syllable. *n.* A unit of pronunciation, normally corresponding to the vowel sounds of a word.

syllepsis. *See* zeugma.

symploche. *n.* The repetition of the same beginning word or words and the same ending word or words in a succession of clauses. Also symploce. See 2 Corinthians 9:6.

synaesthesia. *n.* A *figure of speech in which two seemingly incompatible words or concepts are linked. The term is sometimes used more narrowly of a figure in which a reference to one of the senses is used in connection with a word or phrase that more accurately corresponds to one of the other senses, as in "sharp words" (touch describing something heard). See Acts 15:39; Hebrews 4:12.

synchoresis. *n.* In rhetoric, a concession (e.g., of the truth of an opponent's argument), in order to retort with greater force and effectiveness. See Philippians 1:15-18.

synchronic. *adj.* Concerned with the state of language at a given time (σύν, "with" + χρόνος, "time"); descriptive. *See also* diachronic, linguistics, prescriptive grammar.

syncope. *n.* The loss of a vowel or a whole syllable from the middle of a word. English examples include the pronunciation of words like *hardening* or *interest*, which both have three syllables but are pronounced as if they have only two.

synecdoche. *n.* A *figure of speech whereby a more inclusive term is used for a less inclusive term, or vice versa, as in "Brazil lost the soccer game," which means that a soccer team from Brazil lost the game. In the expression "all hands on deck," "hands" stands for the whole person. Synecdoche may often be called either "part for the whole" (see 2 Cor 3:15; 9:2) or "whole for a part" (see Col 3:15, 21).

syneresis. *n.* The collapsing of two syllables into one. This can happen to words over time (e.g., the word *righteous* used to have three syllables) or deliberately, as in poetry to maintain correct meter (*beneath* becomes *neath*). Also spelled synaeresis.

synesis. *n.* A construction in which agreement in meaning overrides *agreement in *form.

synoeciosis. *n.* A figure in which diverse things are associated or contrary qualities are used of the same thing.

synonym. *n.* A word that means approximately the same thing, or in certain contexts, exactly the same thing, as another word.

synonymia. *n.* The repetition of a thought in synonymous terms (συν–ωνυμία). See Romans 7:15-16.

synopsis. *n.* A book that displays the *pericopae of the *Synoptic Gospels alongside each other in columns in order to show their parallel nature. It may or may not have a commentary to help the reader appreciate the similarities and the differences. Also called Gospel parallel; sometimes confused with a *harmony.

Synoptic Gospels. *pl. n.* Matthew, Mark and Luke, so named because they narrate a large number of the same stories (often with word-for-word agreement) in the same general order, so that if they are written in parallel columns they can be "seen together" (the meaning of "synoptic").

synoptic parallel. *See* synopsis.

synoptic problem. *n.* The puzzle posed to readers of the *Synoptic Gospels (Matthew, Mark and Luke) as to their literary relationship and whether or not other sources such as *Q were used. The problem was recognized early on (the church fathers disagreed on the issue) because of a great deal of verbal agreement and the similar arrangement of material among the Synoptics.

syntactic categories. *See* parts of speech.

syntactical word. *n.* A word as it appears in a *form other than its *lexical form, *inflected according to its syntactical function.

syntagm. *n.* Any constituent (a word or an idiomatic expression) in a *construction.

syntagmatic relations. *n.* In linguistics, the relationships between constituents in a grammatical *construction.

syntax. *n.* The study of the arrangement of words in phrases, clauses and sentences, and the rules involved in sentence formation.

Syrian Text. *See* Byzantine text-type.

T

tag. *n.* In electronic texts, a *grammatical label that marks a word as being a certain case, tense, etc. Once all the words in a computer corpus are tagged, the text can be searched and analyzed extensively.

Talmud. *n.* The *Mishnah plus commentary (i.e., the *Gemara). The Mishnah plus the Palestinian Gemara is called the *Palestinian or Jerusalem Talmud; the Mishnah plus the Babylonian Gemara is called the *Babylonian Talmud.

target language. *n.* The language into which a *translation is made, as opposed to the *source language. Also called the receptor language.

Targum. *n.* Aramaic translations of and commentary on the Hebrew Bible, which are regularly paraphrastic and interpretive. *pl.* Targumim or Targums.

Tatian. *prop. n.* (ca. A.D. 120-173) A Syrian convert best known for his *harmony of the Gospels (the *Diatessaron).

tautology. *n.* The occurrence of unnecessary and ineffective repetition (τὸ αὐτος λογία, "the same saying"). *See also* pleonasm.

taxis. *n.* In *rhetoric, the arrangement of the parts of an argument.

Teaching of the Twelve Apostles. See Didache.

technical term. *n.* A word or phrase that has specialized meaning, often with a very restricted or particular sense.

telic. *adj.* Denoting purpose. The term is used of infinitives, participles subjunctives and whole clauses. Also referred to as final or purpose.

temporal. *adj.* Of conjunctions, particles, participles and clauses, denoting time or duration.

temporal augment. *n.* The *lengthening of a word-initial vowel (ε becomes η; ο becomes ω) to denote a change in the *tense of verbs.

temporal dative. *See* dative of time.

tendential present. *n.* A present-tense verb that denotes action that is intended, attempted or perhaps even likely to occur. Also called conative present or voluntative present.

Tendenz **criticism.** *n.* The study of a literary work with a view to discerning the intention and biases of an author or tracing common themes or interests of a given period.

Tendenzkritik. *See Tendenz* criticism.

tense. *n.* The *morphological feature of the verb (i.e., based on grammatical *form) that indicates the *aspect and *time of the verbal action. The time element, traditionally, has been understood as secondary in the indicative and lacking in the other moods; some grammarians, however, do not think the tense forms ever signify time (i.e., the tenses do not *grammaticalize time, even in the indicative). The tenses in Greek are the *present, *future, *aorist, *imperfect, *perfect and *pluperfect.

tense formative. *n.* A letter or letters added to a verb in the formation of the various tenses. The tense formatives in Greek appear between the verbal *stem and the *personal ending.

tense stem. *n.* The basic form of a verb as it occurs in a particular tense. Also called principal part.

termination. *See* ending.

testimonium. *n.* An Old Testament quotation cited as a *prooftext for Jesus's messiahship (*pl. testimonia*).

text grammar. *See* discourse analysis.

text-critical. *adj.* Relating to *textual criticism.

text linguistics. *See* discourse analysis.

text-type. *n.* A major grouping of biblical *manuscripts based on textual affinity in a large number of passages. The different text-type names—Alexandrian, Byzantine, Western—were coined based on the supposed origin of the manuscripts. *See also* family.

textual analysis. *See* textual criticism.

textual apparatus. *See* critical apparatus.

textual criticism. *n.* The study of the *manuscript evidence for a written work of which the *original is no longer *extant, with the intent to discern the original text. Textual criticism involves gathering and organizing data, evaluating *variant readings, reconstructing the history of the *transmission of the text and attempting to identify the original text. Also referred to as text-criticism.

textual problem. *n.* A text-critical issue for which there is no obvious solution.

textual variant. *See* variant.

Textus Receptus. *n.* The name given to the edition of the Greek New Testament published by Erasmus in the first part of the sixteenth century and essentially reproduced by a number of others on the European continent, including Stephanus, Théodore de Bèza and Abraham Elzevirs. An edition printed by this last individual, in 1633, included a remark in the preface about this form of the text being "commonly received"—and the name stuck (i.e., the Received Text). Prior to this, in 1611, the translators of the King James Version relied heavily on this form of the text. The term is sometimes used loosely as a synonym for the Byzantine text form that stands behind the Textus Receptus. Commonly confused with the Majority Text (*see* Byzantine text-type).

thematic conjugation. *n.* The large group of verbs that *decline similarly because of the presence of a thematic vowel (*see* connecting vowel) that adheres to the *root of a verb and drives the inflectional pattern. Also referred to as omega verbs because of the typical *ending of the first person singular active form.

thematic role. *n.* In linguistics, a semantic role (e.g., agent, source, goal); the relationship between the verb and the noun phrases of a sentence. Also known as the theta role.

thematic verb. *See* thematic conjugation.

thematic vowel. *See* connecting vowel.

Theodotion. *n.* The traditional name of a Greek version of the Old Testament that is either a revision of the *Septuagint or a more literal translation of the Hebrew. It is in the same text tradition as the *Kaige recension and was used widely by the church fathers of the third and fourth centuries (*see* Hexapla). Little is known of the man for whom this version is named; some think he was a proselyte Jew who lived in the last half of the second century A.D.

theological passive. *See* divine passive.

theologoumenon. *n.* A mere deduction reached by theological reasoning from accepted religious truths; or more broadly of any theological content.

theta role. *n.* *See* thematic role.

third attributive position. *n.* The position of an adjective when it appears in the sequence noun-article-adjective.

third class condition. *n.* A *conditional sentence in which the premise of the *protasis (the "if" clause) is presented as uncertain of fulfillment. This is conveyed by using ἐάν plus the subjunctive mood in the protasis and any mood or tense in the *apodosis (the "then" clause). Also called more probable future condition.

third declension. *n.* The inflectional pattern (*see* inflection) for words whose *stems end in α or η.

thoroughgoing eclecticism. *See* rigorous eclecticism.

time. *n.* The feature of language whereby the time of the verbal action is indicated. Traditionally time in Greek has been understood as intrinsic to the *tense system in the indicative mood (called *absolute tense). That is, an indicative verb's tense denotes both *aspect and time. However, some think that time is established by other grammatical features or at the level of the sentence, paragraph or discourse by various means.

timeless. *adj.* Not restricted by temporality.

tmesis. *n.* The separation of the parts of a *compound word by intervening words.

tone syllable. *See* tonic syllable.

tonic syllable. *n.* The syllable that receives the most prominent stress in a word. Also called the tone syllable.

topic. *n.* The person, thing, etc. about which something is said in a sentence (what is said is the *comment). Also known as the *subject.

topos. *n.* Place, space, source, (τόπος, *pl.* τόποι). In Greek rhetoric, the term was used of categories of virtues and vices, of types or methods of argumentation, and of types of figures. In modern *literary criticism, it refers to a traditional or perhaps stereotypical concept or *motif that has become the common possession of a culture or at least a particular segment of a society through its cultural and literary tradition.

Toposforschung. Germ. "topos research." *See* topos.

tradent. *n.* A person or group of persons who preserve and transmit a tradition (Lat. "traditionist"). Also *Trägerkreis.*

traditio. Lat. "transmission" —*n.* The process of transmitting traditional material.

traditio-historical criticism. An attempt to translate the German term *Traditionsgeschichte. See* tradition criticism.

tradition criticism. *n.* The discipline concerned with both the oral and compositional stages in the development of the Gospel material until their fixed form, including the attempt to determine authenticity of material by means of certain criteria. Confusion can arise because both form and *redaction criticism overlap with tradition criticism. Further-more, insofar as *form criticism is used in historical analysis, it approx-imates tradition criticism.

tradition history. *See* tradition criticism.

Traditionsgeschichte. Germ. "tradition history." *See* tradition criticism.

traditum. Lat. "tradition." —*n.* Material that is preserved and transmit-ted.

traductio. *n.* A type of *pun involving different meanings of the same word, or different words with the same spelling. See Romans 8:2-3.

Trägerkreis. See tradent.

transcriptional evidence. *n.* Evidence for a textual critical issue pertain-ing to the practices of *copyists (*scribes) and editors.

transcriptional probability. *n.* The likelihood of a *copyist, in transmis-sion, doing one thing over another (e.g., a type of mistake), which pro-vides a basis for *text-critical decisions. In short, scribes are said to have had a tendency to make difficult wording smooth, terse expres-sions fuller and vague phrases more explicit.

transitive. *adj.* Of verbs, requiring a *direct object. The verbal action is not restricted to the *subject but "goes over" to the direct object (Lat. *transire*, "to go over"). See 1 Corinthians 7:38. *See also* intransitive.

transitive sentence. *n.* A sentence with a *transitive verb as its *main verb.

translate. *v.* To convey in another language. *See* translation.

translation. *n.* The act, process or result of transferring something mean-ingful from one language into another (Lat. *trans*, "across" + *ferre*, "to carry").

translation Greek. *n.* The name given to the sort of Greek that is the end result of the *translation process, still resonating with characteristics of the original language. The term was coined to describe the *style of Greek in the *Septuagint (based on Hebrew and *Aramaic) and in the New Testament (portions of which are thought by some to be based on an Aramaic source). Use of the term can also imply that the translator did not possess the degree of facility in the language necessary to achieve a translation free of the *source language's characteristics. This type of claim is usually made with reference to the *Evangelists who are thought to have spoken Aramaic primarily. *See also* Septuagint Greek.

transliteration. *n.* A word that has been rendered in another language by substituting the corresponding letters of the alphabet rather than translating the meaning of the word (Lat. "across letters"). E.g., the word *baptism* is derived by transliteration from βαπτίζω.

transmission. *n.* The passing down of the biblical text through history by means of copying and distributing.

triple tradition. *n.* Material that is common to all three of the Synoptics (approximately 360 verses). *See also* double tradition; Q; synopsis; synoptic problem; Two-Source hypothesis; Four-Source hypothesis.

trope. *n.* A *figure of speech; the use of a word in a way other than its normal meaning (e.g., metaphor, metonymy).

TSKS. *See* Granville Sharp construction.

Tu es Petrus **pericope.** Lat. "You are Peter." A designation for Matthew 16:18-19.

Tugendkatalog. Germ. "catalog of virtues." *See* vice list, ethical list and *Lasterkatalog.*

Two Ways document/tradition. *n.* The first six chapters of *The *Didache*, which contain catechetical teaching of the early church that contrasts the two ways a person can go, either "the way of life" or "the way of death." Because of its Jewish character and its omissions, some have proposed that this section derives from a pre-Christian Jewish tractate.

Two-Document hypothesis. *See* Two-Source hypothesis.

Two-Gospel hypothesis. *See* Griesbach hypothesis.

Two-Source hypothesis. *n.* A proposed solution to the *synoptic problem that asserts that Mark and *Q are the only two fundamental sources used in the production of the *Synoptic Gospels. It is a variation of the *Oxford hypothesis, which suggests both Matthew and Luke had access to other sources (i.e., the *Four-Source hypothesis).

U

Überlieferungs-geschichte. Germ. "history of transmission." *See* tradition criticism.

UBS. *n.* A Greek New Testament, in several editions, published by the United Bible Societies, including in its apparatus only the more significant textual variants (about a fifth of those listed in the *Nestle-Aland text). A wider range of textual evidence for each variant is included, however.

ultima. *n.* The final syllable of a word. The next-to-last syllable is called the penult.

umlaut. *n.* In textual criticism, a *diacritical mark appearing in the margins of some manuscripts (e.g., Codex Vaticanus) that may indicate a textual variant known to the original *copyist.

uncial. *adj.* Designating a formal style of handwriting characterized by large rounded letters, each separated from the next (like capital letters), and found especially in Greek and Latin codices (*see* codex) of literary works from the second to the eighth century. —*n.* This style, or a letter (i.e., a *majuscule) or *manuscript that is written in this style. From the Latin *uncia*, "twelfth" (our word *inch* is derived from it), apparently a reference to the size of the letter compared to *cursive script. Uncial manuscripts are designated in the *critical apparatus by capital letters (e.g., ℵ, A, B, Ψ) or numbers preceded by 0 (e.g., 0170).

uncountable noun. *See* mass noun.

undefined action. *n.* Verbal action that is presented simply and unadorned, as in "Steve walks" or "Linda sleeps." It makes no comment about the precise nature of the verbal action.

undisputed Pauline epistles. *pl. n.* The New Testament letters of Romans, 1 and 2 Corinthians, Galatians, Philippians, 1 Thessalonians and Philemon, so named because the vast majority of scholars judge them to have been written by the apostle Paul. *See also* deutero-Pauline epistles and *Hauptbriefe*.

ungrammatical. *adj.* Deviating from what is normal or "correct" grammatically. Also called ill-formed.

unknown sayings. *See* agraphon.

unmarked meaning. *See* denotation.

unreal condition. *See* second class condition.

unrestricted. *adj.* Of participles and clauses, independent grammatically.

unvoiced. *adj.* Synonymous with *voiceless.

Urevangelium. *n.* A hypothetical Hebrew or *Aramaic document that served as a source in the production of the *Synoptic Gospels (Germ. "original Gospel").

Urmarkus. *n.* A hypothetical, primitive source thought by some to stand behind Mark's Gospel (Germ. "original Mark"). Also *Urmarcus*.

Urtext. *n.* A hypothetical, primitive form of a biblical text that is no longer *extant but can presumably be reconstructed.

V

varia lectio. Lat. "variant reading." *See* variant.

variable vowel. *See* thematic vowel.

variae lectiones. Lat. "variant readings." *See* variant.

varians lectio. Lat. "variant reading." *See* variant.

variant. *n.* In textual criticism, a different wording (or *reading) of a biblical text that is found in a manuscript. There are approximately half a million variants in all the New Testament manuscripts. However, the term is reserved by some to refer to significant or meaningful textual variants. *See* textual problem.

variant reading. *See* variant.

variation-unit. *n.* In textual criticism, a portion of text in which the manuscript tradition presents at least two *variant forms, and in which, after insignificant *readings have been excluded, each variant form has the support of at least two manuscripts.

Vaticanus. *See* Codex Vaticanus.

vaticinium ex eventu. Lat. "prophecy from an outcome." In *biblical criticism, a passage that describes a future event prophetically but is in fact a literary artifice since the early church or the writer/redactor experienced the event (*pl. vaticinia ex eventu*). *See also prophetia post eventum.*

velar. *adj.* Articulated by raising the tongue to the *velum (or soft palate) near the back of the throat. —*n.* A velar speech sound.

vellum. *n.* A prepared animal skin used for writing or drawing on. It is synonymous with *parchment, although vellum usually denotes a higher quality material made from the skins of young animals.

velum. *n.* The soft part of the back of the mouth (behind the hard palate) that serves as the place of articulation for speech sounds like "k" or the "ng" sound in "wing." Also known as the soft palate.

verb. *n.* A word that describes an action or a state of being.

verb phrase. *See* predicate.

verbal. *adj.* Pertaining to or derived from a word or words, or specifically from verbs. —*n.* A nonfinite verb, i.e., a *participle (a verbal adjective) or an *infinitive (a verbal noun).

verbal adjective. *See* participle.

verbal aspect. *See* aspect.

verbal criticism. *n.* In textual criticism, the study of corruptions in *manuscripts. *See also* variant.

verbal noun. *See* infinitive.

vernacular. *adj.* Native, local or nonstandard. —*n.* The native language of a particular country or region (vis-à-vis the *literary language); everyday speech (Lat. *vernaculus*, "domestic, native, indigenous").

versification. *n.* The introduction of verse numbers into the biblical text

version. *n.* In textual criticism, an early translation of the New Testament from Greek into another language (e.g., Arabic, Coptic, Ethiopic, Latin, Slavonic, Syriac).

verso. *n.* The left-hand side of an open codex (Lat. "left"), as opposed to *recto. Also the back of a papyrus leaf.

Vetus Latina. Lat. "*Old Latin."

vice list. *n.* A literary form in which a catalog of sins is presented for exhortational purposes (e.g., Mt 15:19; Rom 13:13; Gal 5:19-21; Col 3:5, 8; 1 Tim 1:9-10; 2 Tim 3:2-4; 1 Pet 2:1; 4:3). *See also* ethical list.

vocalic. *adj.* Of speech sounds, articulated with free passage of air and relatively little constriction (as with vowels). —*n.* A vocalic sound.

vocalic reduplication. *n.* The *lengthening of the initial vowel or diphthong in the formation of the perfect and pluperfect.

vocation story. *See* calling story.

vocative. *n.* The *case used most often for addressing someone (Lat. *vocare*, "to call"). See Luke 4:23; 1 Corinthians 7:16.

voice. *n.* The feature of a verb that expresses its relationship to the subject, whether the action is directed toward the *direct object (*active voice) or toward the subject (*passive voice). Greek also has *middle voice, which is often *reflexive: the action is directed by the subject back toward the subject.

voiced. *adj.* Of speech sounds, articulated with the vocal cords vibrating.

voiceless. *adj.* Of speech sounds, articulated without the vocal cords vibrating.

volitional future. *See* imperatival future.

volitional optative. *See* voluntative optative.

volitive. *See* voluntative.

volitive optative. *See* voluntative optative.

voluntative. *adj.* Pertaining to volition, the expression of a wish, prayer or command. The term is used in connection with the *future tense and with the *optative and *subjunctive moods when the verbal idea approximates the sense of a command. Also referred to as volitive.

voluntative optative. *n.* An optative mood verb that expresses a prayer, hope or wish. Also called the volitional or volitive optative or the optative of obtainable wish. See Romans 3:3-4; 2 Timothy 1:16; 2 Peter 1:2.

voluntative present. *n.* A present-tense verb specifying the will of the subject of the verb but that has not yet come to realization. Also called conative or tendential present. See John 10:32; Acts 26:28; Galatians 5:4.

Vorlage. *n.* A prototype or source document behind a *recension (Germ. "what lies before"); or an underlying tradition.

vowel. *n.* A speech sound that is relatively unimpeded in the throat and mouth.

vowel gradation. *n.* The shifting of vowels as part of the *declension of words in a language, as in *sing, sang, sung.* It is the *synchronic (i.e., at any given time) shifting of vowels. Sometimes used synonymously with *ablaut. *See also* vowel shift.

vowel quality. *n.* The properties of a particular vowel sound that differentiate it from other sounds.

vowel shift. *n.* The shifting of vowels in a language over time (i.e., *diachronic). Sometimes used synonymously with *ablaut. *See also* vowel gradation.

Vulgate. *n.* The Latin *version of the Bible produced at the end of the fourth century by Jerome. The term simply refers to a translation in common use (Lat. *vulgatus,* "common"), and can be used of the Syriac and Coptic versions too.

W

weak verb. *n.* A verb that does not conform to the regular pattern. Synonymous with *irregular verb.

Western Text. *See* Western text-type.

Western text-type. *n.* One of several *text-types thought to be traceable to the West (Italy, Gaul and North Africa) but which also stems from Egypt and regions farther east. Because of the misnomer, some refer to this text-type as "delta" because its principal representative, *Codex Bezae, is signified by the capital letter D.

wholative genitive. *See* partitive genitive.

whole for the part. *See* synecdoche.

witness. *n.* A *manuscript, *translation or quotation that is brought forward as evidence for a particular *text-critical issue.

womanist criticism. *See* feminist criticism.

word borrowing. *n.* The phenomenon of one language taking in a word or expression from another language.

word play. *See* paronomasia.

word sets. *See* cognate.

word-concept fallacy. *n.* The erroneous notion that each word in a language corresponds to a precise concept, one that remains stable in every context. *See also* dynamic equivalence.

word-final. *adj.* Appearing as the last letter in a word.

word-initial. *adj.* Appearing as the first letter in a word.

X, Y, Z

zeugma. *n.* The use of two closely associated words or clauses with a verb that makes sense with only one of them (ζεῦγμα, "yoking together"). E.g., "I gave you milk to drink and not solid food" (1 Corinthians 3:2). Also known as syllepsis. *See* Luke 1:64; 1 Timothy 4:3.

zoomorphism. *n.* The literary device of ascribing to humans or to God actions or characteristics that naturally belong to animals

Abbreviations, Expressions & Sigla

The following list provides some of the more common abbreviations, foreign words and symbols that permeate grammars and exegetical tools. Direct translations (from Latin unless otherwise noted) are written in quotation marks; an equals sign denotes a term's application or its meaning beyond the literal translation. Letters in parentheses indicate either a plural form and the corresponding plural meaning, such as v(v) = verse(s), or a slightly modified form of an abbreviation or word: for example, ptc(p). = ptc. and ptcp., both of which stand for participle. However, variations in form, especially for abbreviations, are legion, including punctuation and capitalization. Readers should consult a book's own list when such is provided, especially with regard to the involved system of abbreviations and sigla in the apparatus of modern critical biblical texts.

= equals, amounts to

§(§) section(s)

A Codex Alexandrinus

א Codex Sinaiticus

a. *ante*, "before"

A.D. *anno Domini*, "in the year of the Lord"

a datu "from the date"

a fortiori "from a stronger [reason or argument]"

a posteriori "from what comes after" = reasoning from effects to causes, inductive(ly)

a priori "from what is before" = reasoning from causes to effects, deductive(ly)

AB Amplified Bible

ab "from"

ab origine "from the origin"

ab ovo "from the beginning [lit. "egg"]"

abl. ablative

abs. absolute(ly)

acc. accusative(s); according

act. active

ad "at, to" = comment on

ad absurdum "to absurdity," to an absurd degree

ad fin. ad finis, "at or near the end"

ad hoc "to this" = for a specific purpose

ad hominem "to the man" = a personal attack

ad infinitum "to infinity" = without limit

ad init. ad initium, "at [or near] the beginning"

ad l(oc). ad locum, "at the place" = at the passage discussed

ad nauseam "to sickness" = to a ridiculous degree

ad rem "to the point" = pertinent

ad valorem "to the value" = in proportion to the value

add. addit, "it adds" or *addunt*, "they add" = usually of a reading added to a manuscript

adj. adjective, adjectival

adv(l). adverb(ial)

al. *alia,* "other"; *alii,* "others"; *aliqui,* "some, any"; *aliquot,* "some, several"

al certe pl. alii certe plurimi, "certainly very many others"

al. fere omn. alii fere omnes, "nearly all others"

al.[40] fere "nearly forty others"

al. longe pl. alii longe plurimi, "very many others by far"

al. omn. alii omnes, "all others"

al. pc. alii pauci, "a few others"

al. pl. alii plurimi, "very many others"

al. sat. mu. alii satis multi, "a significant number of others"

al. vix mu. alii vix multi, "not a great many others"

aliq. aliqui, "some other"

alt. alternate, the other (e.g., a second occurrence)

ANE Ancient Near East

answ. answer

ante "before"

aor. aorist

ap. apud, "in, among" = quoted in, according to

Ap. Lit. Apocalyptic Literature

Apc. Apocalypse

Apoc. Apocrypha; Apocalypse

app. apparatus; appendix

appar. apparently

append. appendix

appos. apposition

approx. approximately

Aq. Aquila's Greek Translation of the Old Testament

Aram. Aramaic

argumentum e silentio "argument from silence" = an attempt to deduce something based on what a text *does not* say

art. article

ASV American Standard Version

Att. Attic

augm. augment

aut "or"

auth. author

author. authorities

AV Authorized Version

B Codex Vaticanus

b. born; bar (Aram.)/ben (Heb.) "son of"; Babylonian Gemara

B.C. before Christ

B.C.E. before [the] common era (same period as B.C.)

beg. beginning

betw. between

bibl. biblical

Bibl. Aram. Biblical Aramaic

bibliog. bibliography

bis "twice" = used to indicate a double occurrence of a word in a single verse

bk. book

BLE Bible in Living English

Byz Byzantine = supported by the majority of later, Byzantine manuscripts

C Codex Ephraemi Syri

c. *cum,* "with" = supported by; *circa,* "about"; century; column

C.E. common era (same period as A.D.)

ca. *circa,* "about, approximately"

c(ent). century

cet(t). ceteri, "the rest, the other(s)"

cf. *confer,* "confer, compare"

ch(s). chapter(s)

chap(s). chapter(s)

circa "about, approximately"

cj. conjecture

cl. classical; clause

cod(d). codex, -ices; manuscript(s)

codd. ap. Or codices known to Origen

cogn. cognate

col(s). column(s)

comm(s). commentary, -ies

comma "clause, phrase"

commts. commentaries

comp. compound(ed); compiled, -ation, -iler

compar. comparative, -ison

cond. conditional

coniung. coniungo, "join together"

conj. conjunction

consec. consecutive

const(r). construct(ion)

cont(d). continued

contr. contract(ed)

contra "in contrast to"
cor(r). corrector, corrected
corr. corresponding(ly)
Copt. Coptic
correl. correlative
cum "with"
D Codex Bezae
d. died
dat. dative
de facto "of fact" = in reality; in existence
de novo "from new" = starting again, from the beginning
def. defectus, "lacking"
def. definite; definition
del. delere, "to delete, destroy" = deleted, destroyed, effaced
demonstr. demonstrative
dep. deponent
deriv. derived, -atïve
desideratum "a thing desired" = a thing lacked but thought to be necessary
diff. different, differs from
dim(in). diminutive
dir. direct
dir. disc. direct discourse
disc. discussion
diss. dissertation
DSS Dead Sea Scrolls
E Codex Basiliensis
e. Evangelist, gospel(s)
e. ex, "from" = source
e.g. *exempli gratia,* "for example"
ead. eadem, "likewise, the same way"
ed(d/s). editor(s), edition(s), or edited by
editio princeps "first edition"
ellipt. elliptical
emph. emphasis, -atic, -ize, etc.
en masse [Fr.] "in mass" = altogether, as a group, as one
encl. enclitic
Eng. English
enim "for, for instance, because"
ep(s). epistle(s); episode(s)
epex. epexegetical
equiv. equivalent
ergo "therefore"
err. error

esp. especially
ET English translation
et *etiam,* "also, besides, even"
et al. *et alii,* "and others"
et passim "and elsewhere"
etc. *et cetera,* "and the rest"
Eth. Ethiopic
euph. euphemism, -istic(ally)
EV(V) English version(s)
evl. gospel
ex(x). example(s)
ex cathedra "from the chair" = pronouncement from a Pope (also figuratively)
exc. except
excl. excluding
excrpt. excerpt
exp. expanded
expl. explain, -tion, -able, etc.
expr. express, -es, -ing, -ion
extrabibl. extrabiblical
F Codex Borelianus
f(f). and the following one(s)
f(em). feminine
fere "almost, nearly, about"
Festschr. [Germ.] *Festschrift,* "celebratory publication"
fig. figure; figurative(ly)
fin. *finis,* "at or near the end"; finite
fl. *floruit,* "flourished"
fluct. *fluctuare,* "to fluctuate, vary" = the manuscript evidence varies
fol(s). leaf (leaves), folio(s)
foll. follow(s), -ed, -ing,
fort. fortasse, "perhaps, possibly"
Fr. French
fr. from
frag. fragment(s)
freq. frequent(ly)
frg(g/s). fragment(s)
FS [Germ.] *Festschrift,* "celebratory publication"
fut. future
G Codex Boernerianus
gen. genitive, -ival
gener. general(ly)
Ger. German
Gk. Greek
h.l. [Gk.] *hapax legomenon* = sole occurrence

hab. habet, "it has," or *habent,* "they have"

hap. leg. [Gk.] *hapax legomenon* = sole occurence

hapaxl. [Gk.] *hapax legomenon* = sole occurence

HB Hebrew Bible

Heb(r). Hebrew; Hebraism

Hel. Hellenistic

hiat. hiatus, "a cleft, opening" = lacking

hic "this"

i.e. *id est,* "that is"

i.q. *idem quod,* "the same as, equivalent to"

ib. *ibidem,* "in the same place"

ibid. *ibidem,* "in the same place"

id. *idem,* "the same"

idem "the same"

immed. immediately

imp. imperfect

imper. imperative

imperf. imperfect

impers. impersonal

impf. imperfect

impv(l). imperative, (-al)

in. initium, "beginning" = beginning of a verse or reading

in l(oc). in loco, "in the place or passage"

in limine "on the threshold, at the outset"

in loc. cit. in loco citato, "in the place cited"

in ovo "at the inception [lit. "egg"]"

in situ "in position," = in the original place or arrangement

in toto "in all, completely, altogether"

in vacuo "in empty space"

incl. inclusive, include, -ing

ind. indicative

indef. indefinite

indic. indicative

indir. indirect(ly)

indir. disc. indirect discourse

inf. infinitive, -al; *infra,* "below"

infin. infinitive, -al

info. information

infra "below"

init. initium, "at [or near] the beginning"

inscr. inscription

instr. instrumental

int(erp). interpretation (e.g., the Latin translation of the work)

inter alia "among others"

interrog. interrogative

intrans. intransitive(ly)

intro(d). introduce, -ing, -tion

ipse dixit "he himself said [it]" = a dictum; an unproved assertion; a dogmatic statement

ipsissima mens "the very mind"

ipsissima verba "the very words"

ipsissima vox "the very voice"

ipso facto "by the fact itself"

irreg. irregular

Isr. Israelite

ita "so, thus"

item "likewise, also, thus"

j. Jerusalem or Palestinian Gemara

JB The Jerusalem Bible

Jos. Josephus

KJV King James Version

Knox R. A. Knox's translation of the Bible

κτλ. καὶ τὰ λοιπάς, "and the rest" = *et cetera*

l lectionary

l(ib). book

l(l). line(s)

l.c. loco citato, "passage cited"

Lat. Latin

LB Living Bible

lect. lectionary, -ies (i.e., a concensus of lectionaries)

lectio non fluctuat "the reading does not vary"

leg. legit, "it reads" or *legunt,* "they read"

lit. literal(ly)

LIV Living Bible

ll.cc. from *loco citato,* "passages cited"

loanw. loanword

loc. locative

loc. "place(s), location(s)" = in this place

loc. cit. loco citato, "in the place already cited"

LXX Septuagint

𝕸 occuring in the majority of manuscripts

M Mishnah

M.S. *manus secunda,* "second hand"

magnum opus "great work" = the most important work in a career

maj. majority

mal. male, "badly" = they express it badly

marg. margin; marginal reading

m(asc). masculine

metri causa "for the sake of meter"

mg. margin(al)

MGr. modern Greek

Mid(r). Midrash

mid. middle

MLB Modern Living Bible

mn(s). manuscript(s)

mng. meaning

Mod. Gr. modern Greek

modus "manner, mode"

Moffatt J. Moffatt's *A New Translation of the Bible*

mrg. marginal reading

MS(S) manuscript(s)

MT Masoretic Text

mu(lt). multi, "many"

n. note (endnote or footnote); noun

N.B. *nota bene,* "note well" = note carefully

n.d. no date

n.p. no publisher; no place; no page

n.s. new series

NAB New American Bible

NAS(B) New American Standard (Bible)

NEB New English Bible

nec. necessary, -ily

neg. negative

neut. neuter

NHC Nag Hammadi Codex

NIV New International Version

NKJV New King James Version

NLB New Living Bible

nn. notes (footnotes or endnotes)

no(s). number(s)

nom. nominative; nominal

non "not"

nonnul(l). nonnullus, "some, several"

novum "new"

NRSV New Revised Standard Version

NS new series

NT New Testament

num. number

numerus "number"

NWT New World Translation

o.s. old series

obj. object

obs. obsolete

obv. obverse (front side)

occ. occasionally

occidentalis "Western"

oft. often

OL Old Latin

om. omit(s), -ed

omn. omnis, "all" = all manuscripts read

op. cit. opere citato, "in the work cited"

opp. opposite

opp. to opposed to

opt. *optimus,* "the best"; optative

orig. original(ly)

OS old series

OT Old Testament

otherw. otherwise

P. papyrus

p. *post,* "after"; page; Pauline corpus

p(p). page(s)

pace = with due respect to, but differing from

Pal. Palestinian

pap. papyrus

par(s). parallel(s); paragraph(s)

pari pasu "with equal step," equally, simultaneously, side by side, without preference

part. participle

partic. particular(ly)

partim "in part, mostly"

pass. passive

passim "here and there, throughout, everywhere"

patr. fathers, patristic writings

pauc. pauci, "a few"

pc. pauci, "a few"

pecul. peculiar(ly)

per. person; personal

perf. perfect, -ive

perh. perhaps

periphr. periphrastic

permulti "many"

pers. person(s); personal

petitio principii "assuming a principle" = begging the question

pf. perfect, -ive

Phillips J. B. Phillips, *The New Testament in Modern English*

phr. phrase

pl(er). plerique, "very many"

pl(s). plate(s)

pl(ur). plural, plurality

pl. plurimus, "most"

plane "completely"

plpf. pluperfect

plup. pluperfect

plus "more"

pm. *permulti,* "many"

PN personal name; predicate nominative

pon. ponere, "place, put"

poss. possible, -bly; possessive

possess. possessive

post(ea) "after, following, afterwards"

postbibl. postbiblical

pr. primus, "first [occurrence]"; preceding

praem. = a reading that precedes

praeterea furthermore, besides

prec. preceding

pred. predicate

pref. prefix

prep. preposition(al)

pres. present

presc. prescript

prev. previous(ly)

prima facie "at first sight" = at first glance, before closer examination

pro forma "by form" = satisfying only minimum requirements

pro tem pro tempore, "for the time [being]" = temporarily

prob. probable, -bly

pron. pronoun

prov. proverbial(ly)

pseud. pseydonym(ous)

Pseudep. Pseudepigrapha

pt(s). part(s)

ptc(p). participle, -ial

punct. punctuation

Q [Germ.] *Quelle,* "source"

q.v. quod vide, "which see" = used to direct the reader to further information

QED *See quod erat demonstrandum*

qq.v. plural of *q.v.*

qt. quoted by

quid pro quo "something for something" = a fair exchange

quod erat demonstrandum "that which was necessary to prove" = used to state that a proof has just been completed

quot. quotation

R redactor

R(ab). rabbi, rabbinic

r. root; redactor

raison d'être [Fr.] "reason for existing"

re. regarding

REB Revised English Bible

rec(s). recension(s)

recto "right hand page"

ref(f). refer(s), -ence(s), -ing

reflex. reflexive(ly)

reg. regular(ly); register

rel(at.) relative

rel(l). reliquus, "remaining" = the remaining witness(es)

rep(r). represent(s); reprint, -ed

resp. respectively

rev. revised (by), revision; reverse (back)

Rom. Roman

RSV Revised Standard Version

RV(mg) Revised Version (margin)

s.v.(v.) sub verbo, "under the [relevant] word(s), or entry"

saec. saeculum, "century"

saep. saepe, "often"

sc(il). scilicet, "evidently, one may understand" = that is to say, namely, supply

schol. scholium, scholia = marginal comments

scriptio defectiva, "defective writing"

sec. section

sec. secundum, "according to" or "the second occurrence"

sed "but"

sem. semel, "only once"

Sem. Semitic

seq. sequens, "the next, and the following"

ser. series

sg. singular

sic "thus"

signif. signify, -ificant(ly)

sim. similar(ly)

sine "without"

sine qua non "without which nothing" = the indispensable ingredient

sing. singular

sive . . . sive "either . . . or"

solum "alone"

somet. sometimes

specif. specific(ally)

sq(q). sequens = following, the next verse(s)

sth. something

sts. sometimes

sub(st). substantive, -al

subj. subjunctive; subject

subord. subordinate

suf. suffix

substl. substantival

sui generis "of its own kind" = unique, peculiar

sup. *supra,* "above" = previous

superl. superlative

supp(l). supply, supplement

supra "above" = previous

sy. Syriac

Symm. Symmachus's Greek translation of the Old Testament

syn. synonym (-ous)

synop. Synoptic Gospels

Syr. Syriac

t. text (where a marginal reading differs)

t.t. technical term

tant. tantum, "only so much" = this alone, not including any added words

TC textual criticism

tert. tertius, "third"

tertium non datur "a third is not given"

tertium quid "a third something"

TEV Today's English Version

text = text, as opposed to a marginal reading or an accompanying commentary

Tg(s). Targum(s); Targumic

Theod. Theodotion's Greek translation of the Old Testament

theol. theology; *Theologie, theologisch*

tot. totus, "the whole"

TR Textus Receptus

tr. translator, translated by

trans. transitive; translation; translator

transl. translate, -tion(s)

translit. transliterated, -ion

tx(t). text

txt? problematic or corrupted text

txt em textual emendation

u. verse

u.i. ut infra, "as below"

u.s. ut supra, "as above"

UBSGT United Bible Societies Greek Text

uel "or"

uers. version

uid. videlicet, "it seems, apparently; namely"

uide "see"

una voce "one voice" = unanimously

unice "solely, alone"

untransl. untranslated

Urschrift(-en) [Germ.] "original text"

usque (ad) "up to, as far as"

usu. usually

ut "as"

utroq. utroque, "both"

V. vide, "see"

v(v). verse(s)

v. videlicet (see vid.); verb; verse

v.l(l). varia lectio, "variant reading(s)"

v.t. verb transitive

vacat. vacatio, "absence, exemption"

var(r). variant(s); various

vb. verb(al)

vel "or"

vers. version

verso "left hand page"

Vg. Vulgate

vid. videlicet, "that is to say, namely"

vid.inf. vide infra, "see below"

vid.sup. vide supra, "see above"

vide "see"

vis-à-vis [Fr.] "face to face" = relative

to; compared with
viz. videlicet = that is to say, namely
voc. vocative
vol(s). volume(s)
vs(s). verse(s); versus
Vul(g). Vulgate
W Codex Washingtonianus

w. with
wd. word
wr. write, -ers, written
writ. writer(s), writing(s)
x number of times